Close-Up
English in Use

STUDENT'S BOOK **B2**

David McKeegan

Australia • Brazil • Japan • Korea • Mexico • Singapore • Spain • United Kingdom • United States

Contents

Unit	Grammar	Vocabulary
1 pages 4–10	present simple; present continuous; stative verbs	phrasal verbs; prepositions; collocations & expressions; words easily confused; word formation; sentence transformation
2 pages 11–16	present perfect simple; present perfect continuous; present perfect simple & present perfect continuous	phrasal verbs; prepositions; collocations & expressions; words easily confused; word formation; sentence transformation
3 pages 17–22	past simple; past continuous; used to & would	phrasal verbs; prepositions; collocations & expressions; words easily confused; word formation; sentence transformation
4 pages 23–27	past simple vs present perfect simple	phrasal verbs; prepositions; collocations & expressions; words easily confused; word formation; sentence transformation
Review 1 pages 28–32	B2 Practice: FCE (Parts 1–4) B2 Practice: ECCE (Grammar & Vocabulary)	
5 pages 33–37	past perfect simple; past perfect continuous	phrasal verbs; prepositions; collocations & expressions; words easily confused; word formation; sentence transformation
6 pages 38–42	past simple vs past perfect (simple & continuous)	phrasal verbs; prepositions; collocations & expressions; words easily confused; word formation; sentence transformation
7 pages 43–49	future simple; be going to; future continuous; future perfect simple; temporals	phrasal verbs; prepositions; collocations & expressions; words easily confused; word formation; sentence transformation
8 pages 50–55	countable nouns; uncountable nouns; quantifiers	phrasal verbs; prepositions; collocations & expressions; words easily confused; word formation; sentence transformation
Review 2 pages 56–60	B2 Practice: FCE (Parts 1–4) B2 Practice: ECCE (Grammar & Vocabulary)	
9 pages 61–67	can & could; may & might; must; should; would; needn't; be able to; have to; mustn't & don't have to	phrasal verbs; prepositions; collocations & expressions; words easily confused; word formation; sentence transformation
10 pages 68–72	may/might have; should have; could have; can't/couldn't have; must have; would have; needn't have	phrasal verbs; prepositions; collocations & expressions; words easily confused; word formation; sentence transformation
11 pages 73–79	gerunds; infinitives; full infinitives; bare infinitives; gerund or infinitive?	phrasal verbs; prepositions; collocations & expressions; words easily confused; word formation; sentence transformation
12 pages 80–84	indirect questions; question tags; negative questions	phrasal verbs; prepositions; collocations & expressions; words easily confused; word formation; sentence transformation
Review 3 pages 85–89	B2 Practice: FCE (Parts 1–4) B2 Practice: ECCE (Grammar & Vocabulary)	

Unit	Grammar	Vocabulary
13 pages 90–95	passive voice: tenses; gerunds, infinitives & modal verbs	phrasal verbs; prepositions; collocations & expressions; words easily confused; word formation; sentence transformation
14 pages 96–100	causative	phrasal verbs; prepositions; collocations & expressions; words easily confused; word formation; sentence transformation
15 pages 101–106	zero conditional; first conditional; second conditional; third conditional	phrasal verbs; prepositions; collocations & expressions; words easily confused; word formation; sentence transformation
16 pages 107–111	mixed conditionals; conditionals without *if*	phrasal verbs; prepositions; collocations & expressions; words easily confused; word formation; sentence transformation
Review 4 pages 112–116	B2 Practice: FCE (Parts 1–4) B2 Practice: ECCE (Grammar & Vocabulary)	
17 pages 117–121	relative clauses: defining, non–defining clauses	phrasal verbs; prepositions; collocations & expressions; words easily confused; word formation; sentence transformation
18 pages 122–126	participle clauses	phrasal verbs; prepositions; collocations & expressions; words easily confused; word formation; sentence transformation
19 pages 127–133	reported speech: statements, changes in time & place, questions, commands & requests	phrasal verbs; prepositions; collocations & expressions; words easily confused; word formation; sentence transformation
20 pages 134–138	reported speech: reporting verbs	phrasal verbs; prepositions; collocations & expressions; words easily confused; word formation; sentence transformation
Review 5 pages 139–143	B2 Practice: FCE (Parts 1–4) B2 Practice: ECCE (Grammar & Vocabulary)	
21 pages 144–149	comparison of adjectives & adverbs; other comparative structures	phrasal verbs; prepositions; collocations & expressions; words easily confused; word formation; sentence transformation
22 pages 150–155	*too, enough, so* & *such*; gradable adjectives; non–gradable adjectives; adjective order	phrasal verbs; prepositions; collocations & expressions; words easily confused; word formation; sentence transformation
23 pages 156–161	*wish* & *if only*; *had better*; *it's (about/ high) time*; *would rather*; *would prefer* & *prefer*	phrasal verbs; prepositions; collocations & expressions; words easily confused; word formation; sentence transformation
24 pages 162–166	*be used to* & *get used to*; inversion	phrasal verbs; prepositions; collocations & expressions; words easily confused; word formation; sentence transformation
Review 6 pages 167–171	B2 Practice: FCE (Parts 1–4) B2 Practice: ECCE (Grammar & Vocabulary)	

Irregular Verbs 172
Phrasal verbs 174
Prepositions 178
Collocations & Expressions 179
Word formation 180

Unit 1

> **Awareness**

1 Which of these sentences are correct (C) and incorrect (I)?

1. Are you believing in ghosts? ___
2. Sally loves reading bestsellers. ___
3. I'm thinking about going to university. ___
4. You're seeming unhappy. What's wrong? ___
5. We live in the countryside. ___
6. I'm not understanding this documentary. ___
7. What do you think about at the moment? ___
8. The train leaves at 9.20. ___
9. The teacher is always shouting at us. ___
10. Oh dear! It rains very heavily now. ___

How many did you get right? ☐

Grammar

Present Simple

Affirmative	Negative	Questions
I/we/you/they work he/she/it work**s**	I/we/you/they **don't** work he/she/it **doesn't** work	**Do** I/we/you/they **work**? **Does** he/she/it **work**?
Short Answers		
Yes, I/we/you/they do. **Yes**, he/she/it does.	**No**, I/we/you/they **don't**. **No**, he/she/it **doesn't**.	

We use the Present Simple for
- facts or general truths.
*The sun **sets** in the west.*
- routines or habits (often with adverbs of frequency).
*Charlotte **rides** her bike to school every day.*
- permanent states.
*Her family **lives** in Germany.*
- timetabled events in the future.
*The train to London **leaves** at 10.30 am on Sunday.*
- narratives (a story, a joke, a plot, sports commentaries, etc).
*Two monkeys **walk** into a bar …*

> **Note**
> Some common time expressions that are often used with the Present Simple are *every day/week/month/summer, every other day, once a week, twice a month, at the weekend, in January, in the morning/afternoon/evening, at night, on Tuesdays, on Friday mornings,* etc.
> *John goes to the gym **twice a week**.*

> **Remember!** We often use adverbs of frequency with the Present Simple. They tell us how often something happens. They come before the main verb, but after the verb *be*.
*Dad **sometimes** helps me with my homework.*
*My basketball team **rarely** loses.*
*Janet is **often** late for her music lessons.*

Some common adverbs of frequency are: *always* (most often), *usually, often, sometimes, rarely/hardly ever/seldom, never* (least often).

Present Continuous

Affirmative	Negative	Questions
I **am** (**'m**) work**ing** he/she/it **is** (**'s**) work**ing** we/you/they **are** (**'re**) work**ing**	I **am** (**'m**) **not** work**ing** he/she/it **is not** (**isn't**) work**ing** we/you/they **are not** (**aren't**) work**ing**	**Am** I work**ing**? **Is** he/she/it work**ing**? **Are** we/you/they work**ing**?
Short Answers		
Yes, I **am**. **Yes**, he/she/it **is**. **Yes**, we/you/they **are**.	**No**, I'm **not**. **No**, he/she/it **isn't**. **No**, we/you/they **aren't**.	

Spelling: ride → rid**ing**, travel → travel**ling**, stu**dy** → stu**dying**

We use the Present Continuous for
- actions that are in progress at the time of speaking.
*Irene **is playing** football at the moment.*
- actions that are in progress around the time of speaking, but not right now.
*I**'m looking** for a new house.*
- situations that are temporary.
*The kids **are staying** with their uncle till Saturday.*
- an annoying habit (often with *always, continually, constantly* and *forever*).
*Our maths teacher **is always forgetting** to mark our homework.*
- what is happening in a picture.
*Two boys **are climbing** a tree.*
- plans and arrangements for the future.
*I**'m going** to the bank this afternoon.*
- situations that are changing or developing in the present.
*Computers **are getting** faster and faster.*

Note

Some common time expressions that are often used with the Present Continuous are *at the moment, now, for the time being, this morning/afternoon/evening/week/month/year, today*, etc.
*Tonya is having a bath **at the moment**.*

Stative Verbs

Some verbs are not usually used in continuous tenses. They are called *stative verbs* because they describe states and not actions. The most common are:
- verbs of emotion: *hate, like, love, need, prefer, want.*
*I don't **like** greedy people.*
- verbs of senses: *feel, hear, see, smell, sound, taste.*
*You **sound** upset, Kevin.*
- verbs which express a state of mind: *believe, doubt, forget, imagine, know, remember, seem, suppose, think, understand.*
*I don't **understand** Spanish.*
- verbs of possession: *belong to, have, own, possess.*
*Simon **owns** three laptops.*
- other verbs: *be, consist, contain, cost, include, mean.*
*Does the price of the room **include** breakfast?*

Some verbs can be both stative verbs and action verbs, but with a different meaning. The most common of these verbs are:

be	Michael **is** very kind to his baby sister. (usual behaviour) The children **are being** very well-behaved. (at the moment; not their normal behaviour)
expect	I **expect** you want to eat now. (expect = think or believe) We**'re expecting** a delivery this morning. (expect = wait for)
have	Imogen **has** a lot of clothes. (have = own/possess) I**'m having** trouble with my maths homework. (have = experience)
look	You **look** happy. What has happened? (look = seem) I**'m looking** for my glasses. (look = search)
taste	This coffee **tastes** strange! (taste = have a particular flavour) I**'m tasting** the sauce in case it needs more sugar. (taste = test the flavour)
think	Do you **think** this is a good film? (think = have an opinion) Mary **is thinking** of changing jobs. (think = consider)
see	I'm sorry, but I don't **see** the point of this. (see = understand) We**'re seeing** Charlie on Thursday. (see = meet)
smell	Mmm! Dinner **smells** great! (smell = have a particular smell) I**'m smelling** the meat because I think it is old. (smell = action of smelling)
weigh	My aunt **weighs** 90 kilos. (weigh = have a particular weight) I**'m weighing** myself in the bathroom. (weigh = measure the weight)

Unit 1

Grammar Exercises

2 Circle the correct words.

1 He **tastes / is tasting** the soup at the moment to see if it needs more salt.
2 They **are visiting / visit** their grandparents every Sunday.
3 What **do you think / are you thinking** the best way to overcome stress is?
4 Please be quiet. I **am trying / try** to concentrate.
5 I can't come with you to the exhibition because I **am seeing / see** an old friend.
6 He **is thinking / thinks** of buying a house in the country.
7 This perfume **smells / is smelling** awful.
8 Jack always **is wearing / wears** a helmet when he rides.
9 That isn't true. I **am not believing / don't believe** it.
10 Martha **stays / is staying** with Jill for the time being.

3 Complete the sentences with the correct form of the Present Simple or Present Continuous of the verbs in brackets.

1 Mrs Owen _____ (receive) a letter from her son every month. He _____ (study) abroad and _____ (never forget) to write to her.
2 When I _____ (go) to the dentist, I _____ (feel) tense.
3 Kate _____ (find) it difficult to remember new words after studying them. She _____ (not seem) to be able to learn them.
4 She _____ (watch) TV at the moment. She _____ (watch) TV every night before she _____ (go) to bed.
5 Jane can't come to the phone because she _____ (wash) her hair. She _____ (wash) her hair every day.
6 _____ (you / always / lock) your windows before you leave?
7 Look! It _____ (snow). It _____ (seldom snow) at this time of year.
8 Jane _____ (see) a doctor about her headaches tomorrow morning.

4 Write questions to the answers.

1 **A:** Where _____?
   B: I usually go to the recording studio at the weekend.
2 **A:** What time _____?
   B: I go to the gym at five o'clock every day.
3 **A:** Where _____?
   B: My sister works in London.
4 **A:** What _____ on Saturday night?
   B: I am going to a lecture on climate change.
5 **A:** _____ with us to the party on Sunday?
   B: No, I am not. I think I will stay at home.
6 **A:** Why _____ that woolly hat?
   B: It was a present from my aunt, and I'm meeting her in five minutes.
7 **A:** _____ a heavy coat?
   B: No, I don't. I only wear a heavy coat when it is cold outside.
8 **A:** What _____ right now?
   B: I am rewriting my history essay.

5 Rewrite the sentences using the question form and then complete the short answers.

1 My parents eat out during the week.
A: _____? B: No, _____.

2 We are going on a demonstration today.
A: _____? B: No, _____.

3 Sheila is sitting her exams in June.
A: _____? B: Yes, _____.

4 It snows in the Sahara desert.
A: _____? B: No, _____.

5 Paul likes chocolate pancakes.
A: _____? B: Yes, _____.

6 He comes home from work at 7 pm.
A: _____? B: No, _____.

6 Find the mistakes and correct the sentences where necessary. Put a tick (✓) below those which do not need correcting.

1 Does Paul cycles to work every day?
_____

2 My mother always telling us not to eat junk food.
_____

3 What time do the last train leave?
_____

4 He is seeing the consultant at 4 pm today.
_____

5 Nobody thinks that John will pass the exam.
_____

6 My brother don't have a job right now.
_____

7 My friend isn't liking her new cardigan.
_____

8 Maria thinks of moving to a new apartment.
_____

7 Complete the sentences with the word that best fits each gap.

1 Why _____ you always borrowing my laptop?
2 We _____ going to the recording studio next week.
3 Kick off for the match _____ at 12.30.
4 My little brother _____ getting taller every month.
5 I'm _____ leaving until this problem is solved.
6 _____ that boy laughing or crying?
7 _____ you appreciate how hard I have been working?
8 That _____ not surprise me at all!

Unit 1   **7**

Unit 1

Vocabulary

Phrasal verbs

8 Match the phrasal verbs to their meanings.

1. get carried away
2. cheer up
3. chill out
4. face up to (sth)
5. fall for (sb)
6. fall out
7. go off (sth/sb)
8. look up to (sb)
9. put up with (sth/sb)
10. show off

a. to quickly become attracted to somebody
b. to stop liking
c. to feel happier, or make somebody feel happier
d. to tolerate
e. to relax
f. to admire and respect
g. to accept a difficult but true situation or fact
h. to try to make other people think you are great by demonstrating your abilities
i. to get too excited about something
j. to have an argument and stop being friends

9 Complete the sentences with the correct form of the phrasal verbs from 8.

1. I wish John would stop _____. He isn't impressing anybody.
2. He _____ her as soon as he met her, and they got married six months later.
3. It's about time you _____ the fact that you'll never be a rock star.
4. I used to like them, but I _____ them after their last CD.
5. Be warned that the new teacher will not _____ bad behaviour in her class.
6. It's been a hard day, so I just want to _____ in front of the TV this evening.
7. Daniel really _____ his older sister. He'd like to be as successful as she is.
8. Mark and Sue _____ last month, and haven't spoken to each other since.
9. The children _____ with their new computer game, and ended up fighting each other.
10. Sonja looks very sad. Let's try to _____ her _____.

Prepositions

10 Circle the correct words.

1. Failing the test is nothing to be ashamed **of / with**.
2. This kind of music really gets **on / up** my nerves.
3. Deep **under / down**, she knew that she had made a mistake.
4. She used to be a keen hockey player, but last year she broke her leg **at / in** two places.
5. I was **with / under** the impression that you didn't approve of violent films.
6. My cousin Sarah has to be **at / to** the airport at five o'clock.

Collocations & Expressions

11 Circle the correct words.

1. Greg's mother thinks his friends are a **wrong / bad** influence on him.
2. John's first girlfriend **broke / cracked** his heart when she left him.
3. I can't **face / head** doing any more work today. I'm going home.
4. He was afraid to go on stage because he didn't want to **make / show** a fool of himself.
5. You should know **more / better** than to try and cheat in an exam!
6. Please **convey / express** my apologies to your mum.

Words easily confused

12 Use the words given to complete the sentences underneath. Make sure the words are in the correct form. Use each word at least once.

1 say   speak   talk   tell
   a He _____ he was going out, but he didn't _____ me where.
   b Actions _____ louder than words.
   c You're _____ nonsense again. Stop _____ lies and start _____ the truth.
   d What language were they _____? I can't _____ the difference between German and Dutch.
   e Sheila _____ us some marvellous stories during her stay.

2 journey   travel   trip   voyage
   a He's away on a business _____ at the moment.
   b Going on a long sea _____ was dangerous at one time.
   c The _____ will be shorter once they've completed the tunnel.
   d _____ is said to broaden the mind.

3 cost   price   value   worth
   a The _____ of living has risen again.
   b It's _____ far more than I paid for it.
   c We can't afford a new washing machine at that _____.
   d These rare stamps are of great _____.

4 blame   error   fault   mistake   wrong
   a I have been sent two DVDs in _____.
   b It is often quite difficult to tell the difference between right and _____.
   c According to her mother, she could do no _____.
   d Try not to make so many _____.
   e You can't put the _____ on me this time.
   f I invited her by _____.
   g My employing her was a(n) _____ of judgement.
   h It's not my _____ you lost your wallet.

Word formation noun → adjective

13 Use the word in capitals to form a word that fits in the gap.

1 When we were camping, we heard a _____ noise coming from the forest. **MYSTERY**
2 I'm sorry, I didn't mean to do that. It was completely _____. **ACCIDENT**
3 It is a good idea to take a _____ approach to solving this problem. **SCIENCE**
4 It is _____ that I will finish this project on time, I'm afraid. **DOUBT**
5 By the time I came home, the children were fast _____. **SLEEP**
6 You shouldn't put so much salt on your food – it's _____. **HEALTH**
7 When we saw him lying there _____, we thought he was dead. **MOTION**
8 That was the most _____ circus act I have ever seen. **SPECTACLE**
9 Those children are so _____ – do they ever relax? **ENERGY**
10 I can't think of any _____ reason why this plan should not work. **PRACTICE**

Unit 1

Sentence transformation

14 Complete the second sentence so that it has a similar meaning to the first sentence, using the word given. Do not change the word given. You must use between two and five words.

1. My brother has the annoying habit of borrowing my socks.
   forever
   My brother _____ my socks.

2. We used to like this café, but then it changed owners.
   went
   We _____ when it changed owners.

3. The temperature is rising every day.
   getting
   It _____ every day.

4. This is a very difficult situation to accept.
   face
   It's difficult _____ to this situation.

5. I thought you enjoyed going for long walks.
   under
   I _____ that you enjoyed going for long walks.

6. The departure time for the Manchester train is 12.45.
   at
   The Manchester train _____ 12.45.

7. It's not your mother's fault that you forgot your homework.
   blame
   Don't _____ forgetting your homework.

8. I'm not going to tolerate this ridiculous behaviour any longer.
   put
   I'm not going to _____ this ridiculous behaviour any longer.

Unit 2

Awareness

1 Which of these sentences are correct (C) and incorrect (I)?

1. He's tired because he's work all day. ___
2. I haven't saw that play yet. ___
3. Where have you been all afternoon? ___
4. Have you ever been bursting into tears in class? ___
5. Stan has competed in a lot of bicycle races. ___
6. This is the first time I haven't been passing a maths test! ___
7. We've been trying to contact you since this morning. ___
8. The prisoner has escaped! ___
9. Sara hasn't been eating octopus ever before. ___
10. Your eyes are red. Have you cried? ___

How many did you get right? ☐

Grammar
Present Perfect Simple

Affirmative	Negative	Questions
I/we/you/they **have ('ve) eaten** he/she/it **has ('s) eaten**	I/we/you/they **have not (haven't) eaten** he/she/it **has not (hasn't) eaten**	**Have** I/we/you/they **eaten**? **Has** he/she/it **eaten**?
Short Answers		
Yes, I/we/you/they **have**. **Yes**, he/she/it **has**.	**No**, I/we/you/they **haven't**. **No**, he/she/it **hasn't**.	

Spelling: walk → walk**ed**, love → lov**ed**, travel → trave**lled**, ti**dy** → ti**died**, play – pla**yed**

We use the Present Perfect Simple
- for something that started in the past and has continued until now.
*We **have worked** here for ten years.*
- for something that happened in the past, but we don't know or we don't say exactly when.
*Susan **has seen** all of the Harry Potter films.*
- for something that happened in the past and has a result that affects the present.
*I'm very hungry because I **haven't eaten** for hours.*
- for an action that has just finished.
*They **have just done** the dishes.*
- for experiences and achievements.
*He **has run** ten marathons.*
- for an action that happened several times or repeatedly in the past.
*We**'ve asked** this question many times before.*
- with superlatives and expressions *the first/second time*.
*It was the best book I **have** ever **read**.*

Remember! We use *have been* when someone has gone somewhere and has now returned, but we use *have gone* when someone has gone somewhere and is still there.
*Jane **has been** to the gym and now she's at work.*
*Jane **has gone** to the gym, so try calling her later.*

Note
Some verbs are irregular and do not follow these spelling rules. See a list of irregular verbs and their past participles on pages 172–173.

Note
Some common time expressions that are often used with the Present Perfect Simple are *already, ever, for, for a long time, for ages, just, never, once, recently, since 2007/June, so far, twice, three times, until now, yet,* etc.
*Have you **ever** been to London?*

Unit 2

Present Perfect Continuous

Affirmative	Negative	Questions
I/we/you/they **have ('ve) been** play**ing** he/she/it **has ('s) been** play**ing**	I/we/you/they **have not (haven't) been** play**ing** he/she/it **has not (hasn't) been** play**ing**	**Have** I/we/you/they **been** play**ing**? **Has** he/she/it **been** play**ing**?
Short Answers		
Yes, I/we/you/they **have**. **Yes**, he/she/it **has**.	**No**, I/we/you/they **haven't**. **No**, he/she/it **hasn't**.	

Spelling: mak**e** → mak**ing**, run → ru**nning**, stu**dy** → stu**dying**

We use the Present Perfect Continuous
• for actions that started in the past and are still in progress now or have happened repeatedly until now.
Henry **has been living** in Spain since June.
• for actions that happened repeatedly in the past and have finished recently, but that have results affecting the present.
Jane has lost weight because she**'s been exercising** every day.
• to emphasise how long actions have been in progress for.
I**'ve been studying** Spanish literature for two years.
• for a recent or unfinished action.
I**'ve been thinking** about you.

Note

Some common time expressions that are often used with the Present Perfect Continuous are *all day/ night/week, for years/a long time/ ages, lately, recently, since*. We can use *How long ...?* with the Present Perfect Continuous in questions and *for (very) long* in questions and negative sentences.
*We've been painting the garage **all day**.*
*Jessie hasn't been living here **for very long**.*

Present Perfect Simple & Present Perfect Continuous

We use the Present Perfect Simple to talk about something we have done or achieved, or an action that is complete. It is also used to say how many times something happened.
Oliver **has lived** in three different countries.

We use the Present Perfect Continuous to talk about how long something has been happening. It is not important whether it has finished or not.
Amy**'s been working** on her project all summer.

Grammar Exercises

2 Circle the correct words.

1 I **haven't been / haven't been going** to a party since Christmas.
2 It **has rained / has been raining** all day. It seems it will never stop!
3 People **have called / have been calling** all morning to complain about the poor service and they are still calling.
4 I **have tried / have been trying** to contact Peter, but his phone is always engaged.
5 He **has flown / has been flying** an aeroplane before, but he doesn't think he can do it now.
6 Someone **has used / has been using** my towel. It's wet.
7 Since the doctor warned him about his poor health, James **has given up / has been giving up** smoking.
8 We **have missed / have been missing** the bus, so we're walking to school.
9 He **has worked / has been working** for this company for 40 years and **has never caused / has never been causing** any trouble.

12

3 Complete the sentences with the correct form of the Present Perfect Simple or Present Perfect Continuous of the verbs in brackets.

1. What's all this mess? What _____ (you / do) all morning?
2. _____ (you / finish) cooking your omelette yet?
3. Where _____ (Kim / be)? I _____ (look) for her all afternoon.
4. How long _____ (they / study) English?
5. Sorry I'm late. _____ (you / wait) long?
6. Ask John if _____ (he / lock) the garage.
7. I _____ (catch) a cold four times this year.
8. _____ (Karen / make) up her mind about the new job?
9. _____ (you / look after) the children all day? You must be exhausted!
10. Who _____ (use) my laptop? They forgot to switch it off again!

4 Write questions to the answers.

1. A: How long _____?
   B: He's been standing outside for ten minutes.
2. A: What _____ this morning?
   B: I haven't done anything.
3. A: How long _____?
   B: I've known Stella for four years.
4. A: What _____ all afternoon?
   B: The boys have been playing basketball all afternoon.
5. A: Where _____?
   B: I haven't hidden your glasses anywhere!
6. A: Why _____?
   B: I've been crying because I've just seen a very sad film.
7. A: _____ my toothbrush?
   B: No, I haven't. I've got my own toothbrush!
8. A: How long _____?
   B: I've been waiting about half an hour.

5 Find the mistakes and correct the sentences where necessary. Put a tick (✓) below those which do not need correcting.

1. Someone has been smoking in here. I can smell cigarette smoke.

2. The house has belonged to the family from 1920.

3. She just left her office.

4. I've been typing three letters so far this morning.

5. It's the first time she is playing golf with us.

6. We've been checking the records, but we haven't finished yet.

7. Tom has been missing the bus, so he'll be late.

8. Her eyes are red because she has cried.

Unit 2

6 Complete the sentences with the word that best fits each gap.
1. Our teacher has _____ marking tests since last week!
2. Have you finished your project _____?
3. Samantha and Mark have been living together _____ nearly three years.
4. This is the first time I have _____ made a speech.
5. I _____ rewritten this essay twice now.
6. We have been coming to this restaurant every Friday _____ it opened in 2011.
7. _____ long have you been trying to access the Internet?
8. I've _____ seen this film! I don't want to watch it again.
9. Has he broken his new toy _____? That was quick!
10. Who _____ been stealing my cheese from the fridge?

Vocabulary

Phrasal verbs

7 Match the phrasal verbs to their meanings.

1. bottle up
2. burst into
3. calm down
4. chicken out
5. freak out
6. burn out
7. finish with
8. get over

a. to suddenly become very afraid or upset
b. to hide strong emotions
c. to recover from an illness or an upsetting situation
d. to suddenly start making a noise, especially laughing or crying
e. to become less excited
f. to end a relationship
g. to become too afraid to do something
h. to become too ill or tired to do any more work

8 Complete the sentences with the correct form of the phrasal verbs from 7.
1. She _____ tears when she heard that she had failed the exam.
2. Steve _____ his girlfriend last month because they kept arguing about money.
3. I was going to jump off the top diving board, but I _____ in the end – it was too high!
4. It is hard to know how Jane is feeling because she always _____ her emotions.
5. I didn't think Harry would mind me borrowing his bike, but he totally _____ because he thought it had been stolen.
6. _____! You shouldn't get so excited about things.
7. I can't do any more homework tonight – I'm completely _____.
8. It took her a long time to _____ her illness.

Prepositions

9 Complete the sentences with these prepositions.

> for   in   on   to

1. I'm not responsible _____ the behaviour of your children!
2. Danielle wasn't sure how to respond _____ her friend's suggestion.
3. You need to stop playing games and focus _____ your exam preparation.
4. Our teacher is very interested _____ Swedish murder mysteries.
5. It's hard to concentrate _____ this reading task while the television is on.
6. Tim had better be careful – he's heading _____ disaster!

Collocations & Expressions

10 Circle the correct words.

1. It was a great film. I was on the **edge / side** of my seat all the way through it.
2. I don't know what to say. I'm at a **miss / loss** for words.
3. Sara realized that she had forgotten to switch the oven off, so she drove home in a **worry / panic** before the cake got burned.
4. His parents are divorced, but they are still on good **terms / friends** with each other.
5. We didn't think we'd enjoy the modern art exhibition, but we went along out of **curiosity / enthusiasm**.
6. I got an emergency appointment with my dentist because I was in absolute **hurt / agony** with toothache.

Words easily confused

11 Use the words given to complete the sentences underneath. Make sure the words are in the correct form. Use each word at least once.

1. **advise   insist   persuade   suggest**
   a. Do you think you can _____ her to lend you her car?
   b. He _____ on staying at the most expensive hotels.
   c. Her dietician _____ her to lose weight slowly.
   d. Lawrence _____ to us that we should leave on Friday night.

2. **client   customer   guest   patient**
   a. The hotel _____ panicked when they heard the alarm go off.
   b. There were only a few _____ waiting to see the doctor.
   c. He's a well-known lawyer whose _____ include showbiz personalities.
   d. In order to attract _____, the shop owner reduced his prices.

3. **pass   spare   spend   waste**
   a. How do you _____ your free time?
   b. Don't _____ time! You've got a lot of work to do.
   c. Can you _____ ten minutes to discuss the new security arrangements?
   d. Time _____ quickly during the holidays.

4. **course   court   pitch   track**
   a. It's one of the best golf _____ I've played on.
   b. I'm afraid all the tennis _____ are booked.
   c. The spectator who ran onto the _____ was removed from the football stadium by police.
   d. Athletes enjoy running on _____ where the spectators are close to the action.

5. **burgle   cheat   rob   steal**
   a. Her flat has been _____ twice this year.
   b. Nobody knows who _____ the video camera.
   c. My business partner tried to _____ me out of my share of the profits.
   d. Banks in Los Angeles are _____ quite frequently.

Unit 2 15

Unit 2

Word formation — adjective → noun

12 Use the word in capitals to form a word that fits in the gap.

1. Our primary concern is for the _____ of the children at this school. **SAFE**
2. Don't lie to me. I want to hear the _____. **TRUE**
3. It's _____ to go swimming in this weather. You'll freeze! **MAD**
4. Do you know the _____ between an adverb and an adjective? **DIFFERENT**
5. Most students suffer from _____ before an important exam. **ANXIOUS**
6. The _____ of mobile apps is increasing all the time. **POPULAR**
7. It takes a lot of _____ to lift your own weight. **STRONG**
8. What's the _____ between London and Manchester? **DISTANT**
9. There was a lot of _____ in the room before the meeting started. **TENSE**
10. You will need to improve your _____ if you want to compete at this level. **FIT**

Sentence transformation

13 Complete the second sentence so that it has a similar meaning to the first sentence, using the word given. Do not change the word given. You must use between two and five words.

1. I didn't know what to say about Maria's bad news.
   loss
   I was _____ about Maria's bad news.

2. The small child suddenly started to cry when he dropped his ice cream.
   burst
   The small child _____ when he dropped his ice cream.

3. I'm glad that you two are friendly with each other.
   terms
   I'm glad that you two _____ with each other.

4. He was going to enter the race, but he got scared.
   chickened
   He _____ entering the race.

5. She ended their relationship on his birthday.
   finished
   She _____ him on his birthday.

6. After we gave him some food, the baby became quieter.
   calmed
   The baby _____ after we gave him some food.

Unit 3

Awareness

1 Which of these sentences are correct (C) and incorrect (I)?

1. We cancelled the party because Tom was ill. ___
2. You didn't went home early, did you? ___
3. Everyone agreed it was a great plan. ___
4. What did you doing at eight o'clock last night? ___
5. I would enjoy this cartoon when I was a child. ___
6. My dad teached me how to ride a motorcycle. ___
7. I was admiring the view when I heard the explosion. ___
8. Dani used to use *Facebook*, but now she uses *Twitter*. ___
9. Did you used to fight with your brother all the time? ___
10. We were training for the marathon last Sunday. ___

How many did you get right? ☐

Grammar

Past Simple

Affirmative	Negative	Questions
I/he/she/it/we/you/they walk**ed**	I/he/she/it/we/you/they **didn't** walk	**Did** I/he/she/it/we/you/they walk?
Short Answers		
Yes, I/he/she/it/we/you/they **did**.	**No**, I/he/she/it/we/you/they **didn't**.	

Spelling: race → rac**ed**, control → control**led**, study → stud**ied**, play → play**ed**

We use the Past Simple for
- something that started and finished in the past.
*Apollo 11 **landed** on the moon in 1969.*
- past routines and habits (often with adverbs of frequency).
*We **often swam** in the river when we were children.*
- past states
*We **loved** living in the countryside.*
- actions that happened one after the other in the past, for example when telling a story.
*He **stood** up, **walked** to the window, and **shouted** into the night.*

> **Note**
> Some verbs are irregular and do not follow these spelling rules. See a list of irregular verbs on pages 172–173.

> **Note**
> Some common time expressions that are often used with the Past Simple are *yesterday, last night/week/month/summer, a week/month/year ago, twice a week, once a month, at the weekend, in March, in the morning/afternoon/evening, at night, on Thursdays, on Monday mornings,* etc.
> *I listened to some great new bands **at the weekend**.*

Past Continuous

Affirmative	Negative	Questions
I/he/she/it **was** walk**ing** we/you/they **were** walk**ing**	I/he/she/it **was not (wasn't)** walk**ing** we/you/they **were not (weren't)** walk**ing**	**Was** I/he/she/it walk**ing**? **Were** we/you/they walk**ing**?
Short Answers		
Yes, I/he/she/it **was**. **Yes**, we/you/they **were**.	**No**, I/he/she/it **wasn't**. **No**, we/you/they **weren't**.	

Spelling: shine → shin**ing**, control → control**ling**, tidy → tid**ying**

Unit 3

We use the Past Continuous for
- actions that were in progress at a specific time in the past.
*Susan **was walking** home at six o'clock this evening.*
- two or more actions that were in progress at the same time in the past.
*Martin **was reading** while Helen **was watching** TV.*
- giving background information in a story.
*It **was raining**, and a strong wind **was blowing**.*
- an action that was in progress in the past that was interrupted by another action.
*Daniel **was still checking** the bill when the waiter **returned** to the table.*
- temporary situations in the past.
*We **were living** in the suburbs of Manchester at the time.*

Used To & Would

We use *used to* + bare infinitive for
- actions that we did regularly in the past, but that we don't do now.
*I **used to collect** plastic dinosaurs.*
- states that existed in the past, but that don't exist now.
*David **used to be** skinny, but now he's quite large.*

We use *would* + bare infinitive for actions that we did regularly in the past, but that we don't do now. We don't use it for past states.
*During the summer holidays, we **would play** cricket every day until sunset.*

Note
Some common time expressions that are often used with the Past Continuous are *while, as, all day/week/month/year, at ten o'clock last night, last Sunday/week/year, this morning,* etc.
*They were arguing about football **this morning**.*

Grammar Exercises

2 Complete the text with the correct form of the Past Simple or Past Continuous of the verbs in brackets.

I **(1)** _____ (walk) along Regent Street when I **(2)** _____ (realise) that a man **(3)** _____ (follow) me. I **(4)** _____ (turn) right and he **(5)** _____ (follow). Whenever I **(6)** _____ (stop), he **(7)** _____ (do), too. I **(8)** _____ (decide) to take the 717 bus from the bus stop just behind me. Just as the bus **(9)** _____ (move) off, I **(10)** _____ (jump) on. The man **(11)** _____ (miss) the bus, but he **(12)** _____ (get) on another 717. I **(13)** _____ (get) off at Leicester Square with lots of other people. He **(14)** _____ (not notice) me getting off the bus. I immediately **(15)** _____ (head) for the nearest police station.

3 Write sentences using the Past Simple, Past Continuous and **when** or **while**.

1 My father / read a newspaper / my mother / cook
_____

2 My sister / do her homework / I / phone her
_____

3 He / talk on the phone / she / read a magazine
_____

4 Pam / paint her room / her friend / arrive
_____

5 I / read a comic / she / burst into the room
_____

6 A lot of people dance / Kate and I / eat snacks
_____

7 The doctor / examine him / the earthquake happen
_____

4 Write answers to the questions using the word in brackets.

1. **A:** Did he say sorry to her? (him)
   B: No, he didn't say sorry to her. He said sorry to him.
2. **A:** Did your mother know about it? (father)
   B: _____
3. **A:** Was the dog barking at a cat? (the postman)
   B: _____
4. **A:** Did she move here three years ago? (four years ago)
   B: _____
5. **A:** Were the children reading their school books? (comics)
   B: _____
6. **A:** Did George accuse you of stealing? (lying)
   B: _____
7. **A:** Was she laughing at a cartoon? (my hair)
   B: _____
8. **A:** Did Graham Bell invent the television? (the telephone)
   B: _____

5 Write questions to the answers.

1. **A:** _____ at nine o'clock last night?
   B: No, I wasn't sleeping. I was reading.
2. **A:** What _____ at ten o'clock this morning?
   B: I was having a bath.
3. **A:** How long _____?
   B: I taught English in Spain for three years.
4. **A:** Where _____?
   B: They were camping on the beach.
5. **A:** Why _____?
   B: I bought a new laptop because my old one was too slow.
6. **A:** What _____?
   B: I was browsing the Internet when the burglars got in.
7. **A:** Why _____?
   B: I didn't tell you the truth because I was afraid.
8. **A:** _____ when your boss came in?
   B: No, I wasn't working when my boss came in!

6 Circle the correct words.

1. He **used to / would** have long hair.
2. My father would **to take / take** us out for a meal on his birthday.
3. Did you use to **get / getting** a lot of pocket money?
4. They **would / were used to** send us a card every Christmas.
5. I **would / used to** understand German when I was a child.
6. When I was at primary school, I **would / use to** go to bed at eight o'clock.
7. My father **would / used to** smoke, but gave up when his doctor told him to.
8. She would **train / to train** five hours a day when she was in the team.

Unit 3 19

Unit 3

7 Complete the sentences with the word that best fits each gap.

1 _____ you hear about the new exhibition at the library?
2 The sun _____ shining brightly when we woke up the next morning.
3 I was composing a song _____ Jane was writing a poem.
4 Did you use _____ enjoy taking penalties when you played football?
5 I watched a documentary about science and _____ I went to bed.
6 _____ didn't you go to school yesterday?
7 _____ long have you been trying to access the Internet?
8 Where did Tina go _____ night?

Vocabulary

Phrasal verbs

8 Match the phrasal verbs to their meanings.

1 call round   a to telephone somebody again
2 call (sb) back   b to discover by accident
3 call off   c to become available to buy
4 call up   d to visit somebody's house
5 come across   e to become lower (in price)
6 come down   f to go somewhere with somebody
7 come along   g to cancel an event
8 come out   h to telephone

9 Complete the sentences with the correct form of the phrasal verbs from 8.

1 We're going to the Lady Gaga concert. Why don't you _____ with us?
2 If I don't answer the first time, _____ me _____ in half an hour.
3 We're very excited that our first CD is _____ next week.
4 She was clearing out the attic when she _____ an old photo of her grandparents.
5 Why don't you _____ Jane and see if she wants to help us decorate the house?
6 I'll _____ to her house this evening.
7 The prices of mobile phones are _____ every month. I'll soon be able to afford one.
8 The football match was _____ because of the snow.

Prepositions

10 Circle the correct words.

1 We cannot lose this match. We must win **at / by / in** all costs.
2 That was **at / by / in** far the dullest book I have ever read in my life.
3 **At / By / In** general, the weather is slightly warmer in the south of England than in the north.
4 I am writing to you **at / by / in** connection with my recent purchase from your website.
5 She learnt the whole song **at / by / in** heart in about ten minutes.
6 The hotel promised us a car **at / by / in** our disposal for the duration of our stay.

Collocations & Expressions

11 Complete the sentences with the correct form of *do* or *build*.

1 Mr Wilson has _____ a reputation as one of the leading experts in nuclear power.
2 Here, drink this tomato juice – it will _____ you good.
3 It has been a real pleasure _____ business with you.
4 Thankfully, the earthquake didn't _____ much damage to our house.
5 The Romans _____ an empire that stretched from the Atlantic to the Middle East.
6 We spent years _____ a good relationship with our neighbours.

Words easily confused

12 Use the words given to complete the sentences underneath. Make sure the words are in the correct form. Use each word at least once.

1 audience   crowd   gang   listener   member   spectator   viewer

   a The police had difficulty in controlling the _____ that had turned up to greet the team at the airport.
   b _____ will be able to take part in their favourite TV game show.
   c Radio 1 _____ should tune in at four o'clock for live commentary of the match.
   d The _____ thoroughly enjoyed the play.
   e Fewer than one thousand _____ saw the game.
   f Every _____ of the jury felt sorry for the defendant.
   g After the robbery, the _____ escaped in a stolen car.

2 artificial   fake   false   imitation

   a Jackets made of _____ leather are much cheaper than those made of genuine leather.
   b There was no fire. It was a(n) _____ alarm.
   c He lost his job when it was discovered that his diploma was a(n) _____.
   d It wasn't a real Ming vase – it was just a cheap _____.

3 achieve   fulfil   manage   succeed

   a She _____ success very early in her career.
   b We _____ to complete the project in one week.
   c Robert never _____ the promise he showed as a young pianist.
   d William _____ in discovering the truth.

4 bargain   chance   occasion   opportunity   situation

   a The offer of a job abroad was a golden _____ for me to make a fresh start.
   b The scarf was a(n) _____ at £10.
   c What are the _____ of you getting a promotion?
   d It was a(n) _____ on which you could speak to your boss on equal terms.
   e We've got a problem to solve, so let's look at the _____, shall we?

Unit 3

Word formation — verb → adjective

13 Use the word in capitals to form a word that fits in the gap.

1 If you weren't so _____ with your spelling, you'd get better marks. — CARE
2 There is an _____ charge if you want breakfast. — ADD
3 It is time for the _____ children to go to bed. — SLEEP
4 Car fumes contain many _____ chemicals which can damage your health. — HARM
5 This is a very violent film, and so completely _____ for young children. — SUIT
6 There are _____ things you can do to reduce your carbon footprint. — VARY
7 A _____ number of people in this country do not have internet access. — SIGNIFY
8 Several _____ companies have agreed to sponsor this project. — LEAD
9 Don is the most _____ person I know – he hates to lose! — COMPETE
10 I can never get _____ enough to sleep well on a long plane journey. — COMFORT

Sentence transformation

14 Complete the second sentence so that it has a similar meaning to the first sentence, using the word given. Do not change the word given. You must use between two and five words.

1 I climbed trees when I was a young boy.
used
When I was a young boy, _____ trees.

2 I'll phone you again later, when I have more time.
call
I'll _____ when I have more time.

3 She cancelled her birthday party when she became ill.
off
When she became ill, she _____ her birthday party.

4 You must do everything you can to succeed tomorrow.
costs
You must succeed _____ tomorrow.

5 I've never seen a film that was nearly as exciting as that one.
far
That _____ the most exciting film I've ever seen.

6 You'll feel better after a walk in the fresh air.
do
A walk in the fresh air _____ good.

7 I found this by accident when I was cleaning your room.
across
I _____ when I was cleaning your room.

8 Every year, wages are getting lower.
coming
Wages are _____ every year.

Unit 4

Awareness

1 Which of these sentences are correct (C) and incorrect (I)?

1 Our cat has disappeared last week. ___
2 Oh no! I've lost my mobile phone. ___
3 She's been being a member of this club for years. ___
4 This band hasn't released a good CD since 2011. ___
5 Joel suffered from headaches since he was four years old. ___
6 Nobody has ever spoke to me like that before. ___
7 We haven't heard from Tom since a long time. ___
8 I've known Charlie for seven years. ___
9 How long ago did you take up badminton? ___
10 I been on holiday to Morocco last summer. ___

How many did you get right? ☐

Grammar

We use the Past Simple for actions that happened at a specified time in the past and for actions or situations that finished in the past.
I **read** an article about space travel last night.
She **worked** in a museum for two years. (but she no longer works there)

We use the Present Perfect Simple for actions that happened at an unspecified time in the past and for actions or situations that began in the past and are still in progress.
Steven **has written** a poem for his girlfriend. (we don't know or don't say when)
The children **have been** at the swimming pool all afternoon. (they are still in the swimming pool)

Grammar Exercises

2 Circle the correct words.

1 Martin **hasn't seen / didn't see** his daughter since Christmas.
2 I **have looked / looked** for my cat for days, but I never found her.
3 It's three years since I **have last gone / last went** to a rock concert.
4 My mother **didn't find / hasn't found** her purse yet.
5 Mrs Black **has taught / taught** computer science last year.
6 She hasn't acted in a film **for / since** two years.
7 She hasn't finished writing her novel **just / yet**.
8 Einstein **developed / has developed** the theory of relativity many years ago.

3 Use the words given to complete the sentences. There may be more than one possible answer.

| ago   already   always   ever   for   just   recently   since   still   yet |

1 I haven't finished decorating the house _____.
2 I have _____ bought a new car. In fact, I have only had it for two weeks.
3 I haven't seen John _____ a while.
4 She started to learn computer programming three years _____.
5 She _____ hasn't finished cooking. The guests have already arrived.
6 We'll have to choose another film. I have _____ seen this one.
7 Have you _____ visited an old castle?
8 My mother has _____ wanted to visit Hawaii.
9 It's ages _____ I last saw you.
10 I have been having terrible headaches _____.

Unit 4 23

Unit 4

4 Find the mistakes and correct the sentences where necessary. Put a tick (✔) below those which do not need correcting.

1 We haven't play football for a long time.

2 It is been three years since I last went on holiday.

3 Nobody has ever spoken to me like that.

4 How long ago did you became captain of the team?

5 We have finish tidying up our room, Mum. Can we go out now?

6 I have lost my wallet last week.

7 We haven't heard from Tom for a long time.

8 My mother has leaved her books at home again.

9 When have you sent the letter? I haven't received it yet.

10 Sheila has written a letter to me two months ago.

5 Complete the sentences with the correct form of the Past Simple or Present Perfect Simple of the verbs in brackets.

1 Sorry, Mum. I _____ (already eat). I am not hungry.
2 Since I _____ (leave) school two years ago, I _____ (not see) Jenny.
3 I _____ (never eat) this kind of food before.
4 James _____ (not start) working yet. He is still studying at university.
5 Anna _____ (not go) to a concert since she _____ (be) 20.
6 **A:** I hear that Barry _____ (buy) a Ferrari.
   B: Yes, he _____ (buy) it last week.
7 **A:** _____ (you / ever fly) a helicopter?
   B: Yes, I _____ (fly) a helicopter when I was in the air force.
8 Jonathan _____ (oversleep) this morning and _____ (miss) his maths exam. He _____ (not do) that before.
9 Last week, Jim _____ (finish) painting one of the best paintings he _____ (ever paint).
10 Anna _____ (go) to live in the country six months ago and _____ (not be) back since then.

6 Circle the correct words.

1 Tina's **been / gone** shopping. She'll be back soon.
2 I've **been / gone** to the art exhibition. Look what I bought!
3 We'd love to go to Australia. We've never **been / gone** anywhere like that before.
4 The children aren't here. They've **been / gone** to the park.
5 Have you ever **been / gone** to a ballet?
6 Dad's **been / gone** jogging. I don't know when he'll be home.

7 Write questions to the answers given.

1 A: _____
   B: I've lived in this town for five years.
2 A: _____
   B: Tom gave up smoking two years ago.
3 A: _____
   B: No, I haven't bought Donna's present yet.
4 A: _____
   B: We camped in the forest last night.
5 A: _____
   B: Tom has coached the basketball team since last summer.
6 A: _____
   B: Yes, the teacher marked our test last night.
7 A: _____
   B: Yes, I have written a film review before.
8 A: _____
   B: No, he hasn't spoken to her yet.

8 Complete the sentences with the word that best fits each gap.

1 I haven't run a marathon _____ I was 18 years old.
2 The last time I had the flu was two years _____.
3 My parents _____ worked hard all their lives.
4 Tom's uncle has lived in the same flat _____ 15 years!
5 Has your band released a CD _____?
6 I've _____ tasted such a spicy curry before.
7 Have the children _____ been to Disneyland?
8 Where has Stefanie _____? Isn't she here?

Vocabulary

Phrasal verbs

9 Match the phrasal verbs to their meanings.

1 call out   a to total, when added together
2 call on   b to shout
3 call for   c to ask
4 call in   d to suggest an idea or plan
5 come to   e to require or demand
6 come up   f (of information) to become available or known
7 come up with   g to visit for a short time usually while on the way to another place
8 come out   h to be mentioned in a conversation

10 Complete the sentences with the correct form of the phrasal verbs from 9.

1 The audience _____ the author of the play to come on stage.
2 Steven has _____ a brilliant idea! Let's go camping.
3 The news has just _____ that the president is going to resign tomorrow.
4 When we lost our dog, we walked around the streets _____ its name.
5 The bill _____ £65.50.
6 I'll _____ at grandma's house on my way to school this morning to see if she is okay.
7 The quality of school dinners _____ at the meeting last week.
8 Running a marathon _____ a high level of fitness and a lot of determination.

Unit 4

Prepositions

11 Circle the correct words.
1. He admitted that he was **at / in / by** fault, and apologised to his boss.
2. The weather is getting warmer day **at / in / by** day.
3. I am very much **at / in / by** favour of teaching children how to program a computer.
4. She said that she found the novel 'unsatisfying' – **at / in / by** other words, she hated it.
5. The price of petrol has increased **at / in / by** 20% in the past six months.
6. If your house is too close to the river, it is **at / in / by** risk of flooding.

Collocations & Expressions

12 Complete the sentences with the correct form of **play** or **save**.
1. We decided to _____ a joke on Maria.
2. You'll _____ a lot of space if you give away some of the books you don't read anymore.
3. I can't _____ any money because I don't earn enough!
4. The Internet _____ an important role in our research for this project.
5. I'm not sure how I'm going to deal with this situation – I'll just have to _____ it by ear.
6. Our brilliant goalkeeper _____ two penalties during the last match.

Words easily confused

13 Use the words given to complete the sentences underneath. Make sure the words are in the correct form. Use each word at least once.

1. **beat   earn   gain   win**
   a. I think we can _____ his team in the final.
   b. She _____ some money at the horse races.
   c. The chairman is said to _____ about £25,000 a month.
   d. Who _____ the match last week?
   e. Sally's mother says she's not losing a daughter, but _____ a son.

2. **forget   leave   lose   miss**
   a. We'll be late if we _____ the early train.
   b. Have you _____ your book at home again?
   c. Could I borrow a pencil? I've _____ mine. It's in my other pencil case.
   d. I can't find my sunglasses anywhere. I suppose I must have _____ them.

3. **deny   refrain   refuse   reject   resist**
   a. How can he _____ losing the ring when he had it last?
   b. Would visitors please _____ from smoking?
   c. I _____ to help people who won't help themselves.
   d. All my job applications have been _____.
   e. Although the cakes looked delicious, I _____ the temptation to eat one.

4. **manner   path   route   way**
   a. Do you know the _____ to the cathedral?
   b. If we go by the shortest _____, we'll get there by midday.
   c. I enjoy walking along the _____ in Sherwood Forest.
   d. She has such a charming _____.

5 origin source stock supply
  a Nobody knows the _____ of the word.
  b I'll check to see if we have the CD in _____.
  c The country's oil _____ were cut off during the war.
  d Explorers couldn't find the _____ of the river.

Word formation noun → verb

14 Use the word in capitals to form a word that fits in the gap.

1 All my CDs are _____ according to musical type. **CLASS**
2 Can you _____ that you were where you say you were last night? **PROOF**
3 Many medical conditions can be _____ by massage. **RELIEF**
4 We _____ students to make use of our excellent library. **COURAGE**
5 I hope you _____ in your ambition to become a professional dancer. **SUCCESS**
6 The newspaper was forced to _____ for printing incorrect information. **APOLOGY**
7 Don't let the dog out, or it will _____ the children. **TERROR**
8 He doesn't like it if you _____ his work. **CRITIC**

Sentence transformation

15 Complete the second sentence so that it has a similar meaning to the first sentence, using the word given. Do not change the word given. You must use between two and five words.

1 She started to live here two years ago.
   for
   She _____ two years.
2 I haven't seen Tonya for three weeks.
   time
   The _____ Tonya was three weeks ago.
3 He approves of recycling glass and paper.
   favour
   He _____ recycling glass and paper.
4 Serena had an interesting idea about the project.
   up
   Serena _____ an interesting idea about the project.
5 There is a danger that you will injure yourself on this climb.
   risk
   You are _____ yourself on this climb.
6 The last time we met was Christmas.
   since
   We _____ Christmas.
7 You were not to blame for the accident.
   fault
   You were _____ for the accident.
8 You need a lot of patience to do this task.
   calls
   This task _____ patience.

Review 1

B2 Practice: FCE

Part 1

For questions 1–12, read the text below and decide which answer (A, B, C or D) best fits each gap. There is an example at the beginning (0).

Stockholm Syndrome

Imagine the following **(0)** ___. A gang of bank **(1)** ___ cannot escape because the police have the building surrounded. Automatically, the **(2)** ___ become hostages, while the criminals **(3)** ___ time deciding what to do. Outside the bank a crowd has gathered together with TV crews providing **(4)** ___ with live coverage of the incident. Experts appear and **(5)** ___ what should be done to avoid a disaster. Back inside the building, a relationship is developing between the hostages and their captors. They start **(6)** ___ each other about themselves and the hostages begin to put the **(7)** ___ for the incident on the police and authorities.

You may think that this is a scene from a Hollywood movie, but you would be **(8)** ___. The phenomenon is **(9)** ___ as 'Stockholm Syndrome' because it was first observed in Stockholm, Sweden. The hostages helped their captors solve any problems they **(10)** ___ up against and had no intention of letting the police harm them. They even stopped the police **(11)** ___ down a door, and protected their captors when they all left the building together.

Nobody knows quite what **(12)** ___ this behaviour, but it seems that the value of communication cannot be overestimated.

0	A condition	(B) situation	C happening	D state
1	A burglars	B thieves	C shoplifters	D robbers
2	A guests	B customers	C buyers	D clients
3	A pass	B spare	C do	D spend
4	A viewers	B spectators	C listeners	D readers
5	A suggest	B insist	C persuade	D convince
6	A talking	B telling	C speaking	D saying
7	A bad	B error	C fault	D blame
8	A false	B wrong	C missing	D off
9	A called	B described	C known	D named
10	A came	B held	C stayed	D moved
11	A breaking	B bursting	C taking	D destroying
12	A causes	B brings	C makes	D sets

Part 2

For questions 13–24, read the text below and think of the word which best fits each gap. Use only one word in each gap. There is an example at the beginning (0).

Some spare time activities

Spare time activities basically fall into two categories: traditional **(0)** _and_ modern. Traditional activities include pastimes such **(13)** _____ collecting and reading while modern activities involve computer games, the Internet and television.

Children often become interested **(14)** _____ collecting when they come **(15)** _____ something their parents or grandparents have collected. Although they are keen **(16)** _____ collecting when they first start, they very often become fed up with it as **(17)** _____ as they reach their late teens. Reading is a leisure activity that develops with parental encouragement. Unlike collecting, reading is a pastime that people hardly **(18)** _____ abandon.

Nowadays **(19)** _____ are many modern activities which are based on modern technology, and it is not unusual to find a teenager's bedroom full **(20)** _____ computer games. While computer games **(21)** _____ considered to be mainly a teenage pastime, surfing the Internet is popular with both teenagers and adults. Another pastime which teenagers have **(22)** _____ common with adults is watching television. It is interesting **(23)** _____ note that none of these activities involve having a discussion about important issues – something which was popular in **(24)** _____ past.

Part 3

For questions 25–34, read the text below. Use the word given in capitals at the end of each line to form a word that fits in the gap in the same line. There is an example at the beginning (0).

Bringing families closer

A recent survey conducted by a leading scientific magazine
has **(0)** _surprisingly_ revealed that home computers do not   SURPRISE
(25) _____ relationships within families. In fact, the opposite   WEAK
is true – they actually bring children and parents together.
There has been a huge **(26)** _____ in the number of parents   GROW
who have become involved in their children's **(27)** _____ activities EDUCATE
on the computer. This appears to **(28)** _____ bonds between family   STRONG
members, as they work and play together on the machines.
One further **(29)** _____ reached in a report based on the survey is   CONCLUDE
that children's **(30)** _____ needs are satisfied. This occurs because COMPETE
children consistently beat their parents at computer-based games.
The survey must come as a great **(31)** _____ to parents, many   RELIEVE
of whom were understandably **(32)** _____ about the wisdom   DOUBT
of having a computer at home. After all, no parent wants their child to become
anti-social and uncommunicative, which has been a common fear up until now.
The result could be that those parents who have so far been **(33)** _____   WILL
to buy a computer may now do so. They no longer have any reason to be
(34) _____ of these tools, which play an increasingly important   SUSPECT
role in modern life.

Review 1 29

Review 1

Part 4

For questions 35–42, complete the second sentence so that it has a similar meaning to the first sentence, using the word given. Do not change the word given. You must use between two and five words, including the word given. Here is an example (0).

Example:

  0 This is my first fishing trip.
    never
    I _____*have never been on*_____ a fishing trip before.

35 I met Sue at university.
    since
    I _____ we were at university.

36 I don't remember Mary being such a difficult person in the past.
    use
    Mary _____ such a difficult person.

37 Barbara was raised in a small village by her grandmother.
    brought
    Barbara's grandmother _____ in a small village.

38 It takes three hours by car to reach the nearest hospital.
    drive
    It is _____ to the nearest hospital.

39 The growth of these plants was very slow in my back garden.
    grow
    These plants _____ in my back garden.

40 I think what she said at the press conference was true.
    truth
    I think _____ at the press conference.

41 She talks nonsense all the time and I can't stand it.
    fed
    I'm _____ nonsense all the time.

42 What caused the machine to stop working this morning?
    break
    Why _____ this morning?

B2 Practice: ECCE

Grammar

For questions 1–20 choose the word or phrase that best completes the sentence or conversation.

1. 'I can't find Simon.'
   'He has ___ to the theatre.'
   A been
   B gone
   C went
   D done

2. My laptop ran out of power an hour ___.
   A ago
   B since
   C away
   D lately

3. Did we ___ go to the same nursery school?
   A would
   B used to
   C use to
   D using to

4. Those jeans ___ too much money!
   A are costing
   B costs
   C is costing
   D cost

5. 'Where's your cousin?'
   'She ___ in Australia at the moment.'
   A studies
   B is studying
   C study
   D is study

6. I ___ your ridiculous story.
   A don't believe
   B not believe
   C 'm not believing
   D don't believing

7. Who's been ___ my cheese?
   A ate
   B eaten
   C eating
   D eat

8. 'Is this a difficult game?'
   'Well, we've ___ got past Level 2.'
   A ever
   B no
   C done
   D never

9. I ___ having a cup of tea when the phone rang.
   A am
   B was
   C will
   D did

10. I hope they ___ arguing again yesterday.
    A wasn't
    B aren't
    C didn't
    D weren't

11. I've been having a lot of bad dreams ___.
    A since
    B recently
    C ever
    D always

12. 'Can I have a sandwich?'
    'Sorry, I've ___ them all.'
    A already eaten
    B just ate
    C still eaten
    D never ate

13. They ___ living in the big city.
    A were loving
    B are loving
    C loved
    D to love

14. ___ you always brush your teeth at night?
    A Are
    B What
    C Why
    D Do

15. Where ___ your father work?
    A is
    B does
    C are
    D do

16. We saw some great shows ___ year.
    A last
    B ago
    C next
    D once

17. 'Do you want to come out?'
    'I haven't finished writing this essay ___.'
    A still
    B ever
    C yet
    D just

18. 'I'm exhausted.'
    '___ you been working all afternoon?'
    A Are
    B Do
    C Did
    D Have

19. Steve ___ basketball for three years.
    A play
    B has played
    C did play
    D is playing

20. We ___ swimming for ages.
    A didn't be
    B weren't
    C haven't
    D haven't been

Review 1 31

Review 1

Vocabulary

For questions 21–40, choose the word or phrase that most appropriately completes the sentence.

21 I can't ___ eating when I'm this ill.
A face
B mouth
C head
D foot

22 She has always ___ up to her older sister.
A watched
B seen
C looked
D heard

23 The audience ___ into applause at the end.
A snapped
B banged
C burst
D popped

24 Calm down! There's no need to ___ out.
A run
B freak
C crash
D flash

25 Stella hates it when people ___ jokes on her.
A tell
B say
C play
D build

26 Why don't you come ___ with us to the park?
A under
B along
C for
D round

27 We don't have a plan, so let's just play it by ___.
A heart
B ear
C nose
D neck

28 You must get into this university at all ___.
A costs
B prices
C events
D possibilities

29 Did you fall ___ with your best friend again?
A over
B for
C out
D in

30 We were on the ___ of our seats all through the film.
A edge
B side
C corner
D top

31 In other ___, I don't want to go out tonight.
A words
B verbs
C ways
D things

32 Don't ___ a fool of yourself!
A show
B do
C mark
D make

33 It will ___ you good to go on holiday.
A do
B make
C give
D be

34 I know this poem by ___.
A head
B mouth
C stomach
D heart

35 You shouldn't ___ up your feelings.
A box
B carton
C pack
D bottle

36 She really gets ___ away when she listens to music.
A brought
B carried
C taken
D pushed

37 It took him years to get ___ the loss of his mother.
A out
B over
C off
D on

38 I've just ___ up with a brilliant plan!
A gone
B made
C ran
D come

39 I'm sorry, we had to ___ off the meeting.
A tell
B make
C call
D come

40 We had to call ___ the TV repair man last night.
A off
B out
C to
D along

Unit 5

Awareness

1 Which of these sentences are correct (C) and incorrect (I)?

1 We had just arrived when the show began. ___
2 The manager hadn't being informed about the problem. ___
3 They had been played non-stop for about four hours. ___
4 Had you been searching for a long time? ___
5 The teacher had been waiting for everyone to calm down. ___
6 She decided not to go because she hadn't been enjoying it last time. ___
7 We had wrote to the company about this before. ___
8 The children had been swimming all morning. ___
9 I hadn't heard about the new head teacher before yesterday. ___
10 He'd been working for age, but he still hadn't finished. ___

How many did you get right? ☐

Grammar

Past Perfect Simple

Affirmative	Negative	Questions
I/he/she/it/we/you/they **had ('d) watched**	I/he/she/it/we/you/they **had not (hadn't) watched**	**Had** I/he/she/it/we/you/they **watched?**
Short Answers		
Yes, I/he/she/it/we/you/they **had.**	**No**, I/he/she/it/we/you/they **hadn't.**	

Spelling: walk → walk**ed**, love → lov**ed**, travel → trave**lled**, stu**dy** → stu**died**, pla**y** → pla**yed**

We use the Past Perfect Simple for an action or situation that finished before another action, situation or time in the past.
*I **had watched** every one of her films before I **interviewed** her.*
*By the time Greg was 16, he **had become** a national swimming champion.*

Note
Some verbs are irregular and do not follow these spelling rules. See a list of irregular verbs and their past participles on pages 172–173.

Note
Some common time expressions that are often used with the Past Perfect Simple are *before, after, when, already, for, for a long time, for ages, just, never, once, since 2009/July, yet*, etc.
*The footballer hadn't played **for a long time** because of his injury.*

Past Perfect Continuous

Affirmative	Negative	Questions
I/he/she/it/we/you/they **had ('d) been read**ing	I/he/she/it/we/you/they **had not (hadn't) been read**ing	**Had** I/he/she/it/we/you/they **been read**ing?
Short Answers		
Yes, I/he/she/it/we/you/they **had.**	**No**, I/he/she/it/we/you/they **hadn't.**	

Spelling: make → ma**king**, run → ru**nning**, ti**dy** → ti**dying**

We use the Past Perfect Continuous
• for actions that started in the past and were still in progress when another action started or when something happened.
*The audience **had been waiting** half an hour before the band came on stage.*
• for actions that were in progress in the past and had an effect on a later action.
*Steve was exhausted because he **had been training** hard all day.*

Note
Some common time expressions that are often used with the Past Perfect Continuous are *all day/night/week, for years/a long time/ages, since*. We can use *How long ...?* with the Past Perfect Continuous in questions and *for (very) long* in questions and negative sentences.
*The spectators had been watching the match show **for ages** before anyone scored.*

Unit 5

Grammar Exercises

2 Circle the correct words.
1. When her parents arrived, she **had done / had been doing** her homework for three hours.
2. As soon as she got home, she realised she **had left / had been leaving** her glasses at work.
3. My brother **had tried / had been trying** to repair the TV for two hours before I called him.
4. Lisa **had never seen / had never been seeing** such a beautiful painting until she went to the Museum of Modern Art.
5. Amanda **had worked / had been working** as a waitress for three years before she became a singer.
6. By the time the film ended, she **had fallen / had been falling** asleep on the sofa.
7. What **had they seen / had they been seeing** that made them so frightened?
8. **Had you lived / Had you been living** in the house for long before the fire destroyed it?

3 Complete the sentences with the correct form of the Past Perfect Simple or Past Perfect Continuous of the verbs in brackets.
1. Mary _____ (study) for ten hours before she went to bed.
2. How long _____ (you / clean) your room for when your mother arrived yesterday?
3. I _____ (drive) for three hours when the accident happened.
4. She told the doctor that she _____ (not sleep) for two nights.
5. Until I found this job, I _____ (search) for almost ten months without success.
6. Until yesterday, he _____ (never ride) a motorbike before.
7. By the time I got to the theatre, the play _____ (start).
8. I _____ (cook) all afternoon, but I still _____ (not finish) by the time our guests arrived.

4 Choose the correct time expression to complete the sentences.
1. She had been waiting for an opportunity like this ___ years.
   a for   b since   c already
2. What exactly had they been doing ___?
   a today   b all day   c next time
3. Mark had never been to a Formula 1 race ___.
   a after   b just   c before
4. ___ I had spoken, I regretted it.
   a As soon as   b While   c Until
5. ___ had the man been following you for?
   a What time   b How long   c When
6. We had ___ met two years before, and we hadn't liked each other then.
   a never   b always   c already

5 Complete the sentences with the word that best fits each gap.
1. By the _____ I was 11, I'd learnt to play five different musical instruments.
2. We hadn't been on holiday _____ a very long time.
3. Tina had _____ eating cakes all afternoon and now she felt ill.
4. _____ you looked under the bed for your laptop before you asked to borrow Simon's?
5. It was a disappointing match. We had been looking forward to it _____ summer.
6. She had done a lot of research _____ she interviewed the professor.
7. No, we _____ brought a first aid kit – that's why we had to drive to the hospital.
8. _____ had they done to deserve such a hard punishment?

6 Write questions to the answers using the Past Perfect Simple or the Past Perfect Continuous.

1 **A:** _____?
   B: I'd been trying to get in touch with her for three months.
2 **A:** _____?
   B: Yes, he had been told about the new deadline.
3 **A:** _____?
   B: She had tried on three pairs of shoes before she found a pair she liked.
4 **A:** _____?
   B: I had been working in the garden.
5 **A:** _____?
   B: No, he hadn't been crying. He'd been sleeping.
6 **A:** _____?
   B: I'd met her twice before.
7 **A:** _____?
   B: She had spoken to him the day before yesterday.
8 **A:** _____?
   B: They had just been to the circus.

7 Find the mistakes and correct the sentences where necessary. Put a tick (✓) below those which do not need correcting.

1 I hadn't sold any paintings since ages.
   _____
2 Maria had been dancing with Paulo all night.
   _____
3 Mum was upset because the twins had been fight again.
   _____
4 How long had it been for he had checked the oil?
   _____
5 Had they been play in the basement again?
   _____
6 We voted after everyone has had the chance to give their opinion.
   _____

Vocabulary

Phrasal verbs

8 Match the phrasal verbs with their meanings.

1 catch on   □   a to receive (criticism or praise)
2 cater to   □   b to circulate or spread
3 come in for   □   c (of time) to pass
4 go around   □   d to provide something that is wanted
5 catch up   □   e to catch (a disease)
6 come down with   □   f to reach somebody in front of you by moving faster than them
7 go ahead   □   g to become popular
8 go by   □   h to start

Unit 5

9 Complete the sentences with the correct form of the phrasal verbs from 8.

1 There is a rumour _____ that you and Carla are having a relationship.
2 The meeting will _____ as planned at 10.30 am tomorrow.
3 The photographer _____ a lot of criticism for his last exhibition.
4 We have tried to _____ all age groups with our new stage show.
5 If we don't walk faster, we'll never _____ with our tour group.
6 Do you think this new trend of tucking your trousers into your socks will _____?
7 She was looking forward to the camping trip, but she _____ the flu.
8 I can't believe that two whole weeks have _____ and there hasn't been any rain!

Prepositions

10 Circle the correct words.

1 Have you ever made a fool of yourself **at / in / by / behind** public?
2 The audience seldom know what goes on **at / in / by / behind** the scenes of a theatre.
3 Success always comes **at / in / by / behind** a price – and that price is usually years of hard work.
4 The police are doing all they can to catch the murderer and put him **at / in / by / behind** bars.
5 Can I talk to you **at / in / by / behind** private? I have something important to tell you.
6 **At / In / By / Behind** all accounts, this is the best film she has ever made.

Collocations & Expressions

11 Complete the sentences with these words.

| break   capture   eyes   filthy   name   reach |

1 I couldn't believe my _____ when I saw the film star getting out of the taxi.
2 To be truly successful, you have to _____ for the stars.
3 My dad is quite a big _____ in the television industry.
4 It is really difficult to _____ her complex personality in just one photo.
5 One day, I intend to become _____ rich and buy a mansion in the country.
6 Working hard is not enough – you need to have a lucky _____ as well.

Words easily confused

12 Use the words given to complete the sentences underneath. Make sure the words are in the correct form. Use each word at least once.

1 | gap   interval   pause   rest |

   a The dog must have escaped through a(n) _____ in the fence.
   b If you're tired, we can have a(n) _____.
   c The film was so bad that we left during the _____.
   d There are _____ in the cassette which give you time to practise your pronunciation.

2 | borrow   hire   lend   rent |

   a Harold denied that I had _____ him the money.
   b We've _____ a villa for the whole summer.
   c If I were you, I wouldn't _____ money from anyone.
   d A surprisingly large number of people _____ private detectives.

3 | amount   extent   number   quantity   range |

   a You can choose from a wide _____ of books at this shop.
   b It's quality not _____ that is important.
   c He has a large _____ of foreign stamps in his collection.
   d I agree with you to some _____, but we differ on a few points.
   e They have a large _____ of money in a Swiss bank account.

4 memorise recall recognise remember remind

a He'd changed so much that I didn't _____ him.
b _____ to switch off the lights when you leave.
c The spy _____ the code and burnt the paper on which it was written.
d _____ me to phone Jack this evening.
e Do you _____ seeing her at the exhibition?

5 crack leak puncture tear

a I rode over a nail and got a _____ in my front tyre.
b There's a _____ in the sleeve, so I can't wear this shirt.
c If the engine is losing oil there must be a _____ somewhere.
d There was a _____ in the wall after the earthquake.

Word formation   verb → noun

13 Use the word in capitals to form a word that fits in the gap.

1	She had never believed in the _____ of ghosts.	EXIST
2	A detailed _____ of the statistics revealed a problem.	ANALYSE
3	This forest is home to a large _____ of birds.	VARY
4	We have not yet received _____ for the work we did for you.	PAY
5	Although he tried, he could not find the _____ to the puzzle.	SOLVE
6	It gives me great _____ to be here tonight.	PLEASE
7	The factory closed, resulting in hundreds of job _____.	LOSE
8	Have you made a _____ about what subjects you want to study next year?	DECIDE
9	My tennis _____ told me I need to practise more.	INSTRUCT
10	Wearing a helmet will reduce the risk of _____ if you have an accident.	INJURE

Sentence transformation

14 Complete the second sentence so that it has a similar meaning to the first sentence, using the word given. Do not change the word given. You must use between two and five words.

1 Mary didn't start eating until all the family had sat down.
   before
   Mary waited until all the family _____ she started eating.

2 When we got home, she was still painting the room.
   finished
   She _____ the room when we arrived.

3 Natalie graduated from university, then travelled around the world.
   after
   Natalie travelled around the world _____ from university.

4 When we were camping last weekend, I caught a cold.
   down
   I _____ a cold when we were camping last weekend.

5 Lots of people praised Terry's essay in the school magazine.
   came
   Terry's essay in the school magazine _____ a lot of praise.

6 When it finally stopped snowing, the match began.
   ahead
   The match _____ it finally stopped snowing.

7 Everybody says this is a terrible novel.
   accounts
   By _____, this is a terrible novel.

8 I saw an elephant out of the train window – it was incredible!
   eyes
   I couldn't _____ when I saw an elephant out of the train window.

Unit 6

Awareness

1 Which of these sentences are correct (C) and incorrect (I)?

1. Dan was in bed for an hour when we got home. ___
2. We never found out what had happened. ___
3. By the time he was 14 he had since become rich. ___
4. Did you been waiting long? ___
5. They were starving because they hadn't had breakfast. ___
6. Had the audience stopped clapping when you left the stage? ___
7. I was annoyed because I had worked hard on the project. ___
8. She opened the fridge to find someone had drink all the milk. ___
9. We hadn't been driving long when we got a puncture. ___
10. They had woke in the night to find their tent had been stolen. ___

How many did you get right? ☐

Grammar

When we want to show in which order actions happened in the past, we use the Past Perfect for the action that happened first in the past and we use the Past Simple for subsequent actions in the past.

He **had been working** as a mechanic when a football agent **discovered** him and signed him to Manchester City. (First, he had been working as a mechanic and then a football agent discovered him.)

Grammar Exercises

2 Circle the correct words.

1. When I **saw / had seen** Bill yesterday, he hadn't sold his car.
2. The airplane **already took off / had already taken off** when we arrived at the airport.
3. As soon as she entered the house, she realised that somebody **broke / had broken** in and stolen all her furniture.
4. When I **arrived / had arrived** at the cinema, my friend Alice had already bought the tickets.
5. After I **painted / had been painting** my room for an hour, I decided to take a break.
6. By the time I **phoned / had phoned** her, she had already arranged to go out.
7. That was the first time I **ever sang / had ever sung** on stage.
8. The moment the plane took off, I realised that I **left / had left** my glasses at home.

3 Complete the sentences with the word that best fits each gap.

1. We _____ not feel like going out the other night.
2. By the time he got to work, his boss _____ left.
3. Tom and Margaret hadn't _____ getting on very well for quite some time.
4. _____ Greta have enough time to finish the job?
5. Where _____ they met before?
6. I didn't want to leave _____ I had shown everyone my new watch.
7. She hadn't been to the hospital _____ the birth of her second child.
8. We had been _____ a lovely time when we realised that we were at the wrong party.

4 Complete the sentences with the correct form of the Past Simple or the Past Perfect Simple or Continuous of the verbs in brackets.

1 The teacher _____ (tell) us that he _____ (teach) for ten years.
2 She _____ (try) to explain why she _____ (lie) to her parents.
3 By the time I _____ (get) to the concert hall, the heavy metal band _____ (play) for over half an hour.
4 I _____ (not start) tidying up my house until all the guests _____ (leave).
5 We _____ (look) for a hotel room since we _____ (arrived) in the city, and we were now exhausted.
6 John _____ (not ride) very long when he _____ (realise) that he _____ (forget) to bring his packed lunch.
7 How long _____ (you / sit) in the garden when it _____ (start) to rain?
8 _____ (you / see) the children when they _____ (get) home last night? They _____ (be) very dirty and really tired! What _____ (they / do)?

5 Complete the sentences with these time expressions.

| already | after | by the time | for | since | until |

1 I started taking driving lessons only _____ I had bought a new car.
2 The train had already left _____ we reached the station.
3 Sheila had been waiting for me _____ four o'clock.
4 They had been trying to solve the problem _____ three hours when they finally found the solution.
5 She had _____ done her homework by the time her friend came to see her.
6 He didn't leave _____ he had paid the bill.

6 Use the prompts to write sentences.

1 Sally not finish painting the room / when / I call her
   _____
2 As soon as / I enter the house / I realise somebody break in
   _____
3 We / not start eating / until / all our guests arrive
   _____
4 By the time / the police arrive / the thieves get away
   _____
5 After / the famous actress win an Oscar / she retire
   _____
6 She not serve dinner / until / all the family come home
   _____
7 Natalie not graduate from university / when / they offer her a job
   _____
8 I finish my homework / by the time / I go to bed
   _____

Unit 6

7 Write questions to the answers using the Past Simple or the Past Perfect Simple or Continuous.

1 A: _____?
   B: I finished my homework an hour ago.
2 A: _____?
   B: Yes, we'd been talking for quite a long time.
3 A: _____?
   B: They had hidden it under the sofa.
4 A: _____?
   B: No, I hadn't heard it before.
5 A: _____?
   B: Yes, I thought it was a good idea at the time.
6 A: _____?
   B: They had been sleeping in the garage.
7 A: _____?
   B: We announced our marriage in June.
8 A: _____?
   B: She was upset because she had lost her ring.

Vocabulary

Phrasal verbs

8 Match the phrasal verbs with their meanings.

1 live up to
2 live for
3 live on
4 look into
5 nose about
6 look down on
7 look up
8 start out

a to look for something which is hidden
b to begin
c to be as good as expected
d to act like you are better than someone
e to have something or someone as the most important thing in your life
f to try to find information about something on the Internet or in a book
g to investigate or examine
h to mainly eat a particular kind of food

9 Complete the sentences with the correct form of the phrasal verbs from 8.

1 The head teacher promised to _____ the accusations of cheating in his school.
2 Tonya thinks she's so great. She _____ everyone!
3 It was a difficult text. I had to _____ lots of the words in the dictionary.
4 Daniel tried very hard to _____ everyone's expectations, and he mostly succeeded.
5 Mum got suspicious when she discovered the cleaner _____ in her desk drawers.
6 My uncle is a famous journalist who _____ at a local newspaper.
7 No wonder you are overweight. You virtually _____ pasta and potatoes!
8 Sally is very passionate about music. In fact, you could say she _____ it.

Prepositions

10 Circle the correct words.

1 I haven't been sleeping well because I've been **on / to / under / without** a lot of pressure.
2 He was not able to do PE that day **on / to / under / without** account of his bad leg.
3 Much **on / to / under / without** our astonishment, we won the match 6–1.
4 Do not worry, we have everything **on / to / under / without** control.
5 Johnny couldn't make it to the ceremony, so his manager accepted the award **on / to / under / without** his behalf.
6 That was **on / to / under / without** a doubt the most terrifying rollercoaster ride I have ever been on.

40

Collocations & Expressions

11 Complete the sentences with these words.

> drop   eye   made   name   stars   value

1 I can't stand it when people name _____. Who do they think they are impressing?
2 Five pounds for two cinema tickets is good _____ for money.
3 Could you keep a(n) _____ on my bag while I go to the bathroom, please?
4 I can't afford a holiday in Barbados! I'm not _____ of money.
5 Jenny has got _____ in her eyes. I'm sure she's going to move to Hollywood soon.
6 He's trying to make a(n) _____ for himself as a film reviewer.

Words easily confused

12 Use the words given to complete the sentences below. Make sure the words are in the correct form. Use each word at least once.

1 > deck   floor   layer   storey

   a The cake had a thin _____ of cream on top.
   b She lives in a three-_____ house.
   c They work in an office on the 50th _____ of a New York skyscraper.
   d There was a swimming pool on nearly every _____ of the ship.

2 > prescription   receipt   recipe   review

   a You can't exchange goods without a _____.
   b The play received excellent _____.
   c I found the _____ for this meal in a magazine.
   d You need a _____ to get this medicine.

3 > charge   fee   payment   reward   tip

   a I won't leave a _____ if I'm not satisfied with the service.
   b A _____ has been offered for information leading to the arrest of the kidnappers.
   c We deliver and install the system at no extra _____.
   d The _____ are so high at that school that few parents can afford to send their children there.
   e Unless we receive _____ within a week, your order will be cancelled.

4 > company   factory   firm   industry

   a She works for a law _____ in the capital.
   b There was a large explosion at the _____ this morning.
   c All the managers here have a _____ car.
   d This country depends heavily on the tourist _____.

5 > court   jury   sentence   trial

   a During the _____, several witnesses made false statements.
   b The _____ consisted of seven men and five women.
   c If we can't agree on a solution, the matter will have to be settled in _____.
   d The blackmailer received a three-year prison _____.

Unit 6   41

Unit 6

Word formation noun → noun

13 Use the word in capitals to form a word that fits in the gap.

1. Sadly, our _____ ended when he divorced my sister. **FRIEND**
2. The world's leading _____ all agree that global warming is real. **SCIENCE**
3. He left school at 16 and got a job in a _____. **BAKER**
4. Some famous journalists started out as _____ on the Internet. **BLOG**
5. In the oral test, the _____ will ask you questions about your life. **EXAM**
6. Green eyes are a common _____ in our family. **CHARACTER**
7. The time has come for _____, not words. **ACT**
8. I have only one _____ of the play: it was incredibly boring. **CRITIC**
9. What _____ are you? **NATION**
10. If you have a(n) _____ it can be difficult to find suitable employment. **ABILITY**

Sentence transformation

14 Complete the second sentence so that it has a similar meaning to the first sentence, using the word given. Do not change the word given. You must use between two and five words.

1. Dad didn't go to bed until my brother had come home.
   waited
   Dad _____ come home before he went to bed.
2. It was the first time our teacher had shouted at us.
   never
   Our teacher _____ before.
3. I hope I don't disappoint everyone.
   live
   I hope _____ expectations.
4. Refer to *Google* if you don't know what I'm talking about.
   up
   If you don't know what I'm talking about, _____ on *Google*.
5. Football is the most important thing in Malcolm's life.
   for
   Malcolm _____ football.
6. Because of her illness, Stella couldn't go to the party.
   account
   Stella couldn't go to the party _____ her illness.
7. That was the best party this year, definitely.
   doubt
   That was _____ the best party this year.
8. The police are investigating the cause of the fire.
   into
   The police _____ the cause of the fire.

Unit 7

Awareness

1 Which of these sentences are correct (C) and incorrect (I)?

1. I've decided I'm not going join the army. ___
2. Will you come this way, please? ___
3. We'll had left this place by the weekend. ___
4. Shall we going to a restaurant this evening? ___
5. By the time you'll get home, you'll be exhausted. ___
6. I think I'll get a taxi home tonight. ___
7. You'll have been working here since two years tomorrow. ___
8. Look out! That dog is going to bite you. ___
9. After I'm going to have a bath, I'm going out. ___
10. He'll be doing his final exam by this time next week. ___

How many did you get right? ☐

Grammar

Future Simple

Affirmative	Negative	Questions
I/he/she/it/we/you/they **will** win	I/he/she/it/we/you/they **will not (won't)** win	**Will** I/he/she/it/we/you/they win?
Short Answers		
Yes, I/he/she/it/we/you/they **will**.	**No**, I/he/she/it/we/you/they **won't**.	

We use the Future Simple
• for decisions made at the time of speaking.
*It's hot in here. I'**ll open** the widow.*
• for predictions.
*Sea levels **will rise** in the future.*
• for promises.
*I'**ll take** you out to dinner tomorrow, I promise.*
• for threats.
*If you don't finish your dinner, I **won't take** you to the cinema.*
• to talk about future facts.
*Our new album **will be** released in May.*
• after verbs like *think, believe, be sure, expect*, etc and words like *probably, maybe*, etc.
*I'm sure the concert **will be** great.*
• to offer to do something for someone.
*I'**ll help** you with that.*
• to ask someone to do something.
***Will** you **make** me a sandwich, please?*

Note

We use *shall* with *I* and *we* in questions or when we want to make a suggestion or an offer.

*Where **shall we** eat?*
***Shall we** have lunch before the match?*
***Shall I** park the car on the street?*

Unit 7

Be Going To

Affirmative	Negative	Questions
I **am** (**'m**) **going to** win he/she/it **is** (**'s**) **going to** win we/you/they **are** (**'re**) **going to** win	I **am** (**'m**) **not going to** win he/she/it **is not** (**isn't**) **going to** win we/you/they **are not** (**aren't**) **going to** win	**Am** I **going to** win? **Is** he/she/it **going to** win? **Are** we/you/they **going to** win?
Short Answers		
Yes, I **am**. **Yes**, he/she/it **is**. **Yes**, we/you/they **are**.	**No**, I'm **not**. **No**, he/she/it **isn't**. **No**, we/you/they **aren't**.	

We use *be going to* for
• future plans.
Jane's going to buy a new car.
• predictions for the near future based on present situations or evidence.
Look at the sky! There's going to be a thunderstorm.

> **Note**
> Some common time expressions that are often used with the Future Simple and *be going to* are *this week/month/summer, tonight, this evening, tomorrow, tomorrow morning/afternoon/night, next week/month/year, at the weekend, in January, in a few minutes/hours/days, on Thursday, on Wednesday morning*, etc.
> *I'll tell you all about my classmate **later**.*

Future Continuous

Affirmative	Negative	Questions
I/he/she/it/we/you/they **will be** work**ing**	I/he/she/it/we/you/they **will not** (**won't**) **be** work**ing**	**Will** I/he/she/it/we/you/they **be** work**ing**?
Short Answers		
Yes, I/he/she/it/we/you/they **will**.	**No**, I/he/she/it/we/you/they **won't**.	

Spelling: dance → danc**ing**, travel → trave**lling**, ti**dy** → ti**dying**

We use the Future Continuous for
• actions that will be in progress at a specific time in the future.
We'll be sleeping at 1 o'clock tomorrow morning.
• plans and arrangements for the future.
*All the parents **will be attending** a meeting about the new head.*

> **Note**
> Some common time expressions that are often used with the Future Continuous are *this time next week/month/summer, this time tomorrow morning/afternoon/night*, etc.
> ***This time tomorrow**, he'll be working in the new office.*

Future Perfect Simple

Affirmative	Negative	Questions
I/he/she/it/we/you/they **will have** work**ed**	I/he/she/it/we/you/they **will not** (**won't**) **have** work**ed**	**Will** I/he/she/it/we/you/they **have** work**ed**?
Short Answers		
Yes, I/he/she/it/we/you/they **will**.	**No**, I/he/she/it/we/you/they **won't**.	

Spelling: walk → walk**ed**, dance → danc**ed**, travel → trave**lled**, ti**dy** → ti**died**, play → play**ed**

We use the Future Perfect Simple to talk about
• something that will be finished by or before a specific time in the future.
*The accountant **will have finished** his calculations **by** tomorrow.*
• the length of time that an action will have lasted for at a point of time in the future.
*They**'ll have been** here for three weeks **by** the end of this month.*

> **Note**
> Some verbs are irregular and do not follow these spelling rules. See a list of irregular verbs and their past participles on pages 172–173.

> **Note**
>
> Some common time expressions that are often used with the Future Perfect Simple are *by the end of the week/month/year, by this time tomorrow, by tomorrow morning/ten o'clock/2013*, etc.
> ***By the end of the year**, we'll have moved to our new house.*

> **Note**
>
> **Note:** Other tenses that describe the future are the Present Simple for timetabled events, and the Present Continuous for plans and arrangements.
> *The train to Manchester **departs** at 11 am.*
> *My sister **is running** for class president next week.*

Temporals

When we use temporals such as *when, before, after, until, once, by the time*, etc to talk about the future, we use them with a present or a present perfect tense. We do not use them with a future tense.
After I've washed the dishes, I'll watch TV.
By the time he gets to work, he'll be soaking wet.

We use the Present Perfect Simple to emphasise that the first action is finished before the other one starts.
You can have a bath when you arrive at the hotel. (You'll arrive at the hotel first, and then you can have a bath)
Once you have bought the ticket, you can go anywhere in the park. (You will buy the ticket and then you will be able to go anywhere in the park.)

Grammar Exercises

2 Circle the correct words.

1. I promise I **will never hurt / won't be hurting** you again.
2. I **will work / will be working** at 9 pm – I won't be home at that time.
3. Wait a minute. I **will get / will be getting** dressed very quickly.
4. Sue **will have been working / will work** here for ten years by the end of the month.
5. Mary **won't eat / won't have eaten**, so let's take her a sandwich.
6. Mum **will be finishing / will have finished** cooking by the time we arrive.
7. When I get home in the afternoon, my brother **will be watching / will watch** his favourite TV programme.
8. Don't forget. The plane **lands / will land** at 7 pm.

3 Complete the sentences with the correct form of the Future Simple or Future Continuous of the verbs in brackets.

1. I _____ (help) you carry the sofa. Don't worry.
2. I think he _____ (be) here soon.
3. Don't call me at 10 pm – I _____ (have) a bath at that time.
4. This time tomorrow I _____ (lie) on a beach in Miami.
5. I really don't know where I _____ (work) this time next year.
6. It's a beautiful island. I'm sure you _____ (enjoy) your holiday there.

Unit 7

4 Complete the sentences with the correct form of the Future Simple or **be going to** of the verbs in brackets.

1 _____ (you / open) the door for me please?
2 I've decided I _____ (resign) from my job next month.
3 Look at the red sky! It _____ (be) a nice day tomorrow.
4 Isn't your TV working? I _____ (have) a look at it for you.
5 I promise I _____ (be) on time this evening.
6 We _____ (play) tennis this evening. The court is booked for 6 pm.

5 Complete the sentences with the correct form of the Future Perfect Simple, Future Perfect Continuous or Future Continuous of the verbs in brackets.

1 By the end of next month, I _____ (sing) in the church choir for ten years.
2 If Gerry is with them, they _____ (talk) about politics.
3 I _____ (work) late this evening, so don't wait up for me.
4 By the year 2050, we _____ (destroy) all of the Earth's rainforests.
5 We _____ (stay) with my aunt until we find another flat.
6 At the end of the academic year, Mr White _____ (teach) geography at this school for thirty years.

6 Choose the correct responses.

1 Can you come shopping with us tomorrow morning?
   a Sorry, but I'll see my dentist tomorrow morning.
   b Sorry, but I'm seeing my dentist tomorrow morning.
2 I'd really like to meet you on Saturday.
   a Great! I'm not doing anything then.
   b Great! I don't do anything then.
3 What are you thinking about?
   a This time tomorrow, I will lie on a beach.
   b This time tomorrow, I'll be lying on a beach.
4 This is the second time you've lied to me.
   a Sorry, Mum. I'll never lie to you again.
   b Sorry, Mum. I won't be lying to you again.
5 Can you give Tom this parcel for me, please?
   a Of course I can. I will have seen Tom today.
   b Of course I can. I am seeing Tom today.
6 Are you reading another book?
   a Yes, I will be finishing it by this evening.
   b Yes, I will have finished it by this evening.

7 Complete the sentences with the word that best fits each gap.

1 I'm going _____ do my maths homework now.
2 By noon, I will _____ painted my room blue.
3 Will you _____ attending the seminar this afternoon?
4 He's not _____ to finish this by six o'clock.
5 _____ Simon going to wear his new trainers this evening?
6 When _____ you have completed your assignment?
7 By the time the meal _____ ready, I'll be starving!
8 Sara will have _____ waiting for hours by now.

Vocabulary

Phrasal verbs

8 Match the phrasal verbs with their meanings.

1 hang out
2 hang up
3 hang on
4 move in
5 move out
6 move on
7 settle down
8 get away

a to go on holiday or a break
b to spend time with somebody socially
c to change the subject you are talking about
d to stop a telephone conversation
e to start living in a place
f to start feeling comfortable in a place
g to wait for a short while
h to leave the place you live in

9 Complete the sentences with the correct form of the phrasal verbs from 8.

1 We _____ of our flat when my little brother was born.
2 Please _____ a minute. I'll see if I can find your order.
3 It took us a while to _____ in our new house, but we really love it now.
4 The Ross family like to try to _____ to the countryside twice a year.
5 He's going to redecorate before he _____ to his new place.
6 Terry is _____ with his friends at the shopping centre.
7 Let's _____ to another subject, shall we?
8 Samantha _____ the phone before we had finished talking!

Prepositions

10 Circle the correct words.

1 One of the advantages **of / among / on** living in the city is that everything you need is nearby.
2 We agreed to buy the house **of / among / on** condition that they lowered the price.
3 London is **of / among / on** the most expensive cities in the world to live in.
4 Sammy got the job as a result **of / among / on** his qualifications and experience.
5 We get our post delivered to us **of / among / on** a daily basis.
6 We didn't like the flat because, **of / among / on** other things, it didn't have any windows.

Collocations & Expressions

11 Complete the sentences with these words.

ghost   hall   home   night on the   paint the   talk of the

1 Let's _____ town red tonight!
2 This town is becoming like a _____ town. Bands don't play here anymore.
3 There's an important council meeting at the town _____ this evening.
4 I really fancy a _____ town. Shall we go to a club tonight?
5 Her new exhibition is the _____ town.
6 It is a very long time since I have returned to my _____ town.

Unit 7

Words easily confused

12 Use the words given to complete the sentences underneath. Make sure the words are in the correct form. Use each word at least once.

1 **annoy   disturb   matter   mind   object**
   a It doesn't _____ what you wear to the party.
   b What really _____ me is the way she acts when she can't get her own way.
   c I don't want to be _____. Please leave me alone.
   d Don _____ to anyone using his tools.
   e Would you _____ helping me with the washing-up?

2 **attendance   attention   care   notice**
   a Jill attracted the waiter's _____ by clicking her fingers.
   b The students took no _____ of the 'No swimming' signs and dived into the lake.
   c Please pay _____ to what I'm saying.
   d These boxes must be handled with _____.
   e Your _____ record in this class is very poor.

3 **approval   attitude   opinion   view**
   a From my point of _____, it's a waste of time.
   b What provoked their hostile _____ towards you?
   c My boss showed her _____ of the way I ran the office by giving me a pay rise.
   d What's your _____ of the new process?

4 **alike   identical   same   similar**
   a The fingerprints found at the scene of the crime are _____ to yours. You're under arrest.
   b He drives the _____ make of car as my father.
   c They get on well together because they're so much _____.
   d Your watch is _____ to the one I have, but mine has a leather strap.

Word formation   adjective → opposite adjective

13 Use the word in capitals to form a word that fits in the gap.

1 We didn't tip the waiter because he was very _____. **POLITE**
2 It is very _____ that he will pass, because he hasn't revised. **LIKELY**
3 You can wear what you like at our office – we are very _____. **FORMAL**
4 If you do anything _____, I will inform the police. **LEGAL**
5 He's so _____ that I don't think he has ever told the truth in his life! **HONEST**
6 It was really _____ of you to let Jim borrow your car – he hasn't got a licence! **RESPONSIBLE**
7 I'm afraid my new hairstyle makes me look rather _____. **ATTRACTIVE**
8 You are the most _____ person I know. I'm surprised you ever achieve anything! **ORGANISED**
9 What a(n) _____ film that was. Incredible! **ORDINARY**
10 Our post gets delivered at such _____ times – we never know when to expect it. **REGULAR**

Sentence transformation

14 Complete the second sentence so that it has a similar meaning to the first sentence, using the word given. Do not change the word given. You must use between two and five words.

1. Our party is on Saturday afternoon at our house.
   having
   We _____ our house on Saturday afternoon.

2. If you don't hurry, we'll arrive after the film starts.
   started
   If you don't hurry, _____ by the time we arrive.

3. I started feeling ill on Monday, and it's now Wednesday.
   have
   By Thursday, I _____ for four days.

4. We never really began to feel comfortable in the village.
   settle
   We never really _____ in the village.

5. They like to go on holiday every Christmas.
   away
   They like to _____ every Christmas.

6. Because of her illness, Stella couldn't go to the party.
   account
   Stella couldn't go to the party _____ her illness.

7. Who do you like to spend time with socially?
   hang
   Who do you _____ with?

8. If you don't like your flatmates, you should leave the flat.
   out
   You should _____ if you don't like your flatmates.

Unit 8

> **Awareness**

1 Which of these sentences are correct (C) and incorrect (I)?

1 Take the rubbishes outside, please. ___
2 There is some good news for you in this letter. ___
3 Hurry up! We don't have many time. ___
4 The police were asking questions about Carol. ___
5 We're still waiting for some new equipments. ___
6 He gave me a useful advice. ___
7 How much brothers do you have? ___
8 Few people go to the theatre these days. ___
9 Can you give me an information, please? ___
10 He didn't invite many friends to the party. ___

How many did you get right? ☐

Grammar

Countable Nouns

Most nouns are countable and have singular and plural forms.
book – books
puppy – puppies
boy – boys
potato – potatoes
leaf – leaves
sheep – sheep
woman – women
foot – feet

We usually use *a* or *an* with singular countable nouns.
a *road*
an *avenue*

We can use *some*, *any* or a number (e.g. *three*) with plural countable nouns.
There are **some** *dogs in the park.*
Are there **any** *flowers in your garden?*
I haven't been to the cinema for **three** *years.*

We use singular or plural verb forms with countable nouns depending on whether we are talking about one or more items.
A *bike* **is** *useful when you live in a big city.*
Lorries are *noisy and cause a lot of congestion.*

> **Remember!** Some countable nouns don't end in *-s*. Remember to use a plural verb form with them.

Women are *safer drivers than men.*
He ran for miles and now his **feet are** *sore.*

Uncountable Nouns

Some nouns are uncountable. They do not have plural forms.

advice	health	music
biology	history	progress
cheese	homework	research
chocolate	information	rubbish
equipment	knowledge	salt
food	luggage	time
fruit	medicine	traffic
fun	milk	water
furniture	money	weather

50

We don't use *a* or *an* with uncountable nouns. We can use *some* and *any*.
I'd like **some** food, please.
I haven't got **any** money with me.

We always use singular verb forms with uncountable nouns.
Music **is** my life.
This medicine **tastes** disgusting.

Remember! Some uncountable nouns end in *-s*. Remember to use a singular verb form with them.
The news this morning **was** shocking.
Maths **is** a difficult subject.

We can use phrases describing quantity with uncountable nouns to say how much we have. The most common of these phrases are:
- *a bag of*
- *a bottle of*
- *a bowl of*
- *a can/tin of*
- *a carton of*
- *a cup/glass of*
- *a jar of*
- *a loaf of*
- *a packet of*
- *a piece of*

I'd like **a bowl** of soup.
There's **a bottle** of water in the fridge.

Quantifiers

We use *some* with both uncountable and plural countable nouns in affirmative sentences and in requests or offers.
I bought **some CDs** this weekend.
Could I have **some advice**, please?
Would you like **some help** to lift that?

We use *any* with both uncountable and plural countable nouns in negative sentences and in questions.
I don't have **any money**.
Have you read **any** good **books** lately?

We use *a lot of/lots of* with both uncountable and plural countable nouns.
Lots of people don't like cabbage.
I have **a lot of rubbish** to get rid of.

We use *a little* with uncountable nouns and *a few* with plural countable nouns in affirmative sentences.
I had **a little sugar** in my coffee this morning.
There were **a few spiders** in my bedroom.

We use *much* with uncountable nouns and *many* with plural countable nouns in negative sentences and in questions.
How **much salt** should I put in this casserole?
There aren't **many cyclists** in this part of the city.

Unit 8

Grammar Exercises

2 Complete the sentences using the plural form of the nouns in brackets.
1 There were some intelligent _____ at the meeting. (man)
2 Scientific _____ are made every day. (discovery)
3 We went to an island with many beautiful _____. (beach)
4 James couldn't reach the top three _____ of the bookcase. (shelf)
5 She saw two _____ under the bed and started screaming. (mouse)
6 She went on a diet because she had put on ten _____. (kilo)
7 Many animal _____ are becoming extinct. (species)
8 Sarah didn't like any of her wedding _____. (photo)
9 We saw some _____, some _____ and some _____. (fox, deer, sheep)
10 I broke two _____ when I fell over. (tooth)

3 Are these nouns Countable or Uncountable? Put them in the correct row.

| baby boy bread brush child coffee damage fun |
| furniture kiss knife music potato shelf water weather |

COUNTABLE	_____ _____ _____ _____
	_____ _____ _____ _____
UNCOUNTABLE	_____ _____ _____ _____
	_____ _____ _____ _____

4 Complete the sentences with **a**, **an**, **some** or **any**.
1 I would like _____ information about the rooms in your hotel.
2 I'd like _____ soup, please.
3 Mum, I need _____ money to buy _____ new notebook.
4 I watched _____ unusual film at the cinema yesterday.
5 We haven't bought _____ new furniture for years!
6 Could you give me _____ advice, please?
7 Could you buy _____ loaf of bread, Tom?
8 I need _____ equipment for my camping holiday.
9 No, thank you. We don't need _____ advertising at the moment.
10 He did _____ damage to his car when he reversed into a building.

5 Match the phrases with the nouns.

1 a piece of ☐   a soup
2 a carton of ☐   b honey
3 a loaf of ☐   c cake
4 a cup of ☐   d tuna
5 a bowl of ☐   e milk
6 a tin of ☐   f coffee
7 a packet of ☐   g crisps
8 a jar of ☐   h bread

6 Complete the sentences with **few, a few, little, a little** or **a lot**.
1 _____ people applied for the job, so they put another advertisement in the newspaper.
2 I have _____ time to watch TV. I have too much work.
3 Jack has _____ of friends in this town. It seems that everybody likes him.
4 I gave my teacher _____ ideas for the class project. He liked them a lot.
5 In _____ years, people will be using the Internet to do their shopping.
6 I have _____ free time today. How about going to the cinema?
7 'Mum, I need _____ of help with this project,' said Sheila.
8 My father has _____ patience with people who are rude to him.

7 Write questions to the answers using **How much** or **How many**.
1 A: _____? B: I've been to France twice.
2 A: _____? B: I have £6.
3 A: _____? B: It's three days to my birthday.
4 A: _____? B: There were 20 people at my party.
5 A: _____? B: It takes a lot of time to learn the piano.
6 A: _____? B: We just need a little sugar.

8 Complete the sentences with the word that best fits each gap.
1 Can I have _____ few of your peanuts, please?
2 There are _____ fresh yoghurts in the fridge.
3 No, thank you. I don't want _____ money.
4 I'm afraid the news _____ not good.
5 There aren't _____ places to play in this town – just a park and the village hall.
6 _____ of students live in this part of the city.
7 The traffic _____ really bad this morning.
8 My feet _____ hurting quite badly at the moment.

Vocabulary

Phrasal verbs

9 Match the phrasal verbs with their meanings.
1 get across ☐   a to have a good relationship with
2 get at ☐   b to stand up
3 get round to ☐   c to finally do something which you meant to do
4 get in ☐   d to be chosen or accepted into an institution
5 get on ☐   e to succeed in making someone understand something
6 get out of ☐   f to succeed in a competition or exam
7 get through ☐   g to avoid doing something which you don't want to do
8 get up ☐   h to be able to reach something

10 Complete the sentences with the correct form of the phrasal verbs from 9.
1 It is important to _____ with your colleagues.
2 I've got lots of homework, and I must _____ doing it before the weekend.
3 Our team _____ the second round of the competition, then we were beaten 4–0.
4 Everyone in the room _____ out of their seats and applauded when he entered the room.
5 Put the biscuits on the top shelf, so that the children can't _____ them.
6 The message I am trying to _____ is 'be safe'.
7 Sammy was very happy when he _____ to his first choice of university.
8 If I can _____ going training tonight, I will. I really don't feel like it.

Unit 8 53

Unit 8

Prepositions

11 Circle the correct words.

1 You can do what you like this weekend **as / for / in** far as I'm concerned.
2 I'm just going to sit here and relax **as / for / in** the moment – then I'll start work.
3 It wasn't such a bad film – **as / for / in** a matter of fact, I really enjoyed it.
4 They used to meet **as / for / in** secret every day after school.
5 Why don't we go somewhere else **as / for / in** a change?
6 Can you put that **as / for / in** writing for me, please?

Collocations & Expressions

12 Complete the sentences with these words.

concrete   lane   life   personal   population   rat

1 There is a shortage of housing in the city because of a recent _____ explosion.
2 The city is sometimes referred to as a _____ jungle.
3 Do you like living life in the fast _____?
4 I hate it when people invade my _____ space.
5 My parents came from very different walks of _____.
6 We moved to the country to escape the _____ race.

Words easily confused

13 Use the words given to complete the sentences underneath. Make sure the words are in the correct form. Use each word at least once.

1 lay   lie   scatter   spread

  a The demonstrators _____ when the riot police appeared.
  b On average our hens _____ one egg a day.
  c The detectives _____ out and searched the field for the murder weapon.
  d Could you help me _____ the table, please?
  e _____ down if you feel unwell.

2 age   period   term   time

  a Her uncle spent two brief _____ working in Asia.
  b In this day and _____, up-to-date information is vital.
  c We get our school reports at the end of _____.
  d Do you remember the _____ when we went to Brands Hatch?
  e We have history first _____ on Monday morning.

3 condition   position   situation   state

  a We've bought a second-hand car in excellent _____.
  b Finding herself in a _____ of power has changed her completely.
  c The _____ got worse and worse until war broke out a year later.
  d Your children are in an excellent _____ of health.

4 damage   harm   injury   pain   wound

  a He still bears the scars of a gunshot _____ on his right leg.
  b A serious back _____ forced him to miss most of last season.
  c Brenda was in quite a lot of _____ after the operation.
  d Fortunately, the storm did little _____ to our property.
  e A little exercise won't do you any _____!

Word formation — adverbs

14 Use the word in capitals to form a word that fits in the gap.

1. When everyone is sitting _____, I will begin. — **COMFORT**
2. If you are not aware of what you are doing, you are acting _____. — **CONSCIOUS**
3. People who speak _____ are never very popular. — **OFFEND**
4. The economy is _____ getting stronger every year. — **STEADY**
5. It was _____ kind of him to give you all that money. — **EXTRAORDINARY**
6. I don't _____ agree with what she says, but she is making sense today. — **GENERAL**
7. Peter drives so _____ that nobody will get in the car with him. — **DANGER**
8. The light comes on _____ when someone enters the room. — **AUTOMATIC**
9. If you didn't work so _____, you wouldn't make so many mistakes. — **CARE**
10. The director made the actors rehearse the scene _____ until it was perfect. — **REPEAT**

Sentence transformation

15 Complete the second sentence so that it has a similar meaning to the first sentence, using the word given. Do not change the word given. You must use between two and five words.

1. Not many students went on the school trip last week.
   few
   There was a school trip last week, but _____ came.

2. We have very little money, so we must be careful.
   much
   We _____ money, so we must be careful.

3. Simon has very few friends in this school.
   many
   Simon _____ friends in this school.

4. I tried, but I couldn't make him understand my concerns.
   across
   I tried, but I couldn't _____ to him.

5. It is impossible to avoid the end-of-term exam.
   get
   You can't _____ the end-of-term exam.

6. My sister and I have a really good relationship.
   well
   My sister and I _____ with each other.

7. I do not mind if they pay me at the end of the month.
   concerned
   As _____ they can pay me at the end of the month.

8. He asked me to write it down.
   put
   He asked me _____ writing.

Unit 8

Review 2

B2 Practice: FCE

Part 1

For questions 1–12, read the text below and decide which answer (A, B, C or D) best fits each gap. There is an example at the beginning (0).

Recycling in the office

One of the most exciting new **(0)** ___ in the field of recycling is a machine that can clean used photocopier paper. The device, **(1)** ___ a decopier, uses a mixture of chemicals to loosen the ink from the paper. A brush then **(2)** ___ the ink, leaving the paper completely clean. **(3)** ___ to the manufacturers, nothing like this has appeared on the **(4)** ___ before. They claim that the machine is **(5)** ___ of cleaning one sheet of paper at least five times. This is because the damage **(6)** ___ to the paper by the cleaning chemicals is compensated for by a special chemical which increases its **(7)** ___.

It is predicted that the machine will **(8)** ___ on despite the high cost. The initial price of £30,000 will be too high for small companies, but they will be able to **(9)** ___ one for a reasonable monthly sum, or wait for a cheaper version to **(10)** ___ out. Multinational companies will have a golden **(11)** ___ to help the environment and will save £30,000 within 18 months. What is more, the machine will, to a great **(12)** ___, provide a way to improve security, as it offers an alternative to shredding confidential documents.

0	A revelations	(B) inventions	C discoveries	D concoctions
1	A called	B named	C known	D described
2	A rejects	B resists	C removes	D refrains
3	A Listening	B Speaking	C Accounting	D According
4	A shops	B store	C business	D market
5	A capable	B able	C possible	D potential
6	A made	B exposed	C inflicted	D done
7	A power	B strength	C health	D fitness
8	A catch	B get	C carry	D bring
9	A take	B lend	C borrow	D rent
10	A come	B bring	C go	D get
11	A chance	B opportunity	C occasion	D possibility
12	A length	B extent	C range	D amount

Part 2

For questions 13–24, read the text below and think of the word which best fits each gap. Use only one word in each gap. There is an example at the beginning (0).

Staying attractive

Many people (0) __find__ it difficult to stay slim. They are disappointed (13) _____ their looks. Soon there may be a solution (14) _____ their problems. Instead of going on diets or working out in the gym, (15) _____ will be possible to take tablets to lose weight or stay young. These tablets will be as easy to take (16) _____ vitamin pills!

Researchers have discovered the protein which is the (17) _____ important in determining whether or not calories are stored as fat. It has (18) _____ found in human tissue, and drugs which increase the amount of this protein are being tested (19) _____ the moment. There is also an 'exercise pill' which will allow the user to lose about one kilo a month without doing any exercise at (20) _____.

The growth hormone HGH is the key to youthful looks. HGH keeps skin (21) _____ becoming 'loose' and stops arteries 'hardening'. Tests show that an increased level of HGH (22) _____ people feel and look much younger. Pharmaceutical companies are going to develop special drugs to cause the body to release more HGH (23) _____ normal to help people hold (24) _____ to their youth.

Part 3

For questions 25–34, read the text below. Use the word given in capitals at the end of each line to form a word that fits in the gap in the same line. There is an example at the beginning (0).

A better place to live

An Italian animal charity recently carried out a very (0) __successful__ operation. They managed to transfer five	SUCCESS
unhappy tigers from an extremely small and (25) _____	COMFORT
cage in Italy to much more (26) _____ surroundings in	LUXURY
England. This is just one of several wonderful examples of	
(27) _____ cooperation between animal welfare	NATIONAL
organisations.	
The tigers' (28) _____ at their new home in Kent has	ARRIVE
brought hope to people whose lives are dedicated to the	
prevention of (29) _____ to animals on a daily basis.	CRUEL
Of course, such happy endings are not always possible.	
(30) _____, not all animals can be liberated from the	FORTUNATE
often desperately (31) _____ conditions in which they	HEALTH
are discovered. There are many reasons for this, but the most common	
one is because of (32) _____ delays in legal procedures	REASON
within the animals' host country. Added to this is the fact that	
many courts are (33) _____ to the needs of animals	SENSE
in captivity. Concern for animal welfare is not the same across	
different cultures. In order to end this (34) _____	NECESSITY
suffering, a greater understanding of the problem must be	
promoted worldwide.	

Review 2

Part 4

For questions 35–42, complete the second sentence so that it has a similar meaning to the first sentence, using the word given. Do not change the word given. You must use between two and five words, including the word given. Here is an example (0).

Example:

0   It is a soldier's duty to obey his superior.
    carry
    A soldier _____*must carry out*_____ his superior's orders.

35 The rent was lower than I had expected.
    as
    The rent _____ I had expected.

36 This is her first chess tournament.
    never
    She _____ chess tournament before.

37 I've never looked after a dog before.
    used
    I _____ after a dog.

38 Harry didn't turn off his stereo when we came in.
    carried
    When we came in, Harry _____ his stereo.

39 His answer to the first question is wrong.
    mistake
    He _____ the first question.

40 She tried as hard as she could, but she failed.
    did
    She _____, but she failed.

41 Karen will never let you pay her share of the bill.
    insists
    Karen _____ her share of the bill.

42 There has been another increase in the price of petrol.
    gone
    The price of petrol _____ again.

B2 Practice: ECCE

Grammar

For questions 1–20, choose the word or phrase that best completes the sentence or the conversation.

1. 'Did you enjoy the concert?'
   'By the time we arrived, the band ___ home.'
   A had went
   B have went
   C had gone
   D have gone

2. They had been waiting ___ five hours.
   A since
   B until
   C yet
   D for

3. She ___ my letter by now.
   A receives
   B will have received
   C will be receiving
   D will receive

4. 'Did Tom and Mark help you with it?'
   'No, we'd finished by the ___ they got here.'
   A hour
   B minute
   C time
   D second

5. ___ you close the window for me, please?
   A Are
   B Do
   C Will
   D Shall

6. She had never tried octopus ___ that day.
   A before
   B for
   C at
   D when

7. It ___ the first time she had driven a fast car.
   A was
   B is
   C had been
   D did

8. Does the soup need ___ more salt?
   A a little
   B a few
   C many
   D a lot of

9. Shall we just try and calm down ___ a moment?
   A for
   B at
   C with
   D by

10. '___ we go out tonight?'
    'I don't really feel like it.'
    A Are
    B Shall
    C Have
    D Do

11. After I ___ lunch, I'm going to bed.
    A will have
    B am having
    C have
    D had

12. I'd like ___ cheese and biscuits, please.
    A any
    B few
    C some
    D much

13. ___ you been informed about the meeting before it happened?
    A Have
    B Did
    C Had
    D Will

14. What are you ___ to study at university?
    A want
    B will
    C having
    D going

15. I was late because someone had ___ my car keys.
    A hided
    B hidden
    C hiding
    D hide

16. You ___ left by the time I arrive, won't you?
    A will
    B have
    C going to
    D will have

17. 'Why haven't the twins called?'
    'Don't worry. They ___ at Grandma's house yet.'
    A don't arrive
    B won't arrive
    C won't have arrived
    D hadn't arrived

18. 'How about some chocolate cake?'
    'OK, thanks. But not too ___.'
    A many
    B lots
    C much
    D few

19. What ___ to deserve such strong punishment?
    A had they done
    B did they
    C will they have done
    D do they

20. Sorry, but I haven't got ___ cash.
    A no
    B none
    C some
    D any

Review 2

Vocabulary

For questions 21–40, choose the word or phrase that most appropriately completes the sentence.

21 I'll __ into the possibility of forming a computer club.
   A see
   B hide
   C watch
   D look

22 Who has been __ around in my room?
   A eyeing
   B nosing
   C mouthing
   D facing

23 I still haven't got __ to writing to my mother.
   A over
   B round
   C up
   D through

24 That was delicious! Can I have the __?
   A receipt
   B review
   C recipe
   D prescription

25 It's a nice idea, but I don't think it will __ on.
   A take
   B have
   C catch
   D bring

26 As a __ of fact, I do care about you.
   A thing
   B matter
   C figure
   D concept

27 Please __ on a minute – I just need to finish this call.
   A wait
   B hang
   C move
   D stay

28 Why does he look __ on people?
   A up
   B over
   C down
   D round

29 Stanley has already made a __ for himself at university.
   A face
   B name
   C man
   D title

30 Koala bears __ on eucalyptus leaves.
   A eat
   B drink
   C are
   D live

31 His latest novel __ in for a lot of harsh criticism.
   A came
   B went
   C ran
   D fell

32 We're never going to catch __ with them – they're too fast.
   A down
   B up
   C along
   D on

33 As far as I'm __, he can do what he wants.
   A cared
   B concerned
   C known
   D bothered

34 Greg has been __ a lot of pressure.
   A on
   B at
   C under
   D over

35 The meeting was held __ private.
   A to
   B on
   C under
   D in

36 It's a great restaurant, by all __.
   A stories
   B sayings
   C bills
   D accounts

37 Let's __ somewhere for the weekend.
   A get away
   B go along
   C get around
   D go over

38 I don't think that meal was good __ for money.
   A value
   B cost
   C price
   D cash

39 I didn't understand the point he was trying to get __ to us.
   A in
   B on
   C across
   D at

40 We really __ the town red last night!
   A painted
   B coloured
   C brushed
   D covered

60

Unit 9

Awareness

1 Which of these sentences are correct (C) and incorrect (I)?

1. We must to finish this by the end of the day. ___
2. You don't have to bring your computer to school. ___
3. They shouldn't eating so much cake. ___
4. He might be right about that. ___
5. Tonya ought join an athletics club. ___
6. Could you be explain this problem to me, please? ___
7. She needn't type out the whole report. ___
8. May I borrow your laptop? ___
9. Would you talking more quietly, please? ___
10. You should try to get some sleep. ___

How many did you get right? ☐

Grammar

Can & Could

We use *can* + bare infinitive
• to talk about general ability in the present and the future.
He **can write** his name, and he's only two!
• for requests.
Can you **fix** my bike?
• for permission.
Ok, you **can leave** the room.

We use *can't* + bare infinitive to show that we are sure that something isn't true.
He **can't be** a policeman; he looks too young.

We use *could* + bare infinitive
• to talk about general ability in the past. (past form of *can*)
My brother **could ride** a bike when he was three.
• to talk about possibility.
Don't ride on the pavement – you **could hurt** a pedestrian.
• for polite requests.
Could you **help** me lift this suitcase on to the rack, please?
• to make suggestions.
You **could try** adding a few more spices.

May & Might

We use *may* + bare infinitive
• to talk about possibility in the future.
Daniel **may decide** that he doesn't want to go to college.
• for polite requests. (with *I* and *we*)
May we **join** you at your table this evening?
• for polite permission.
Yes, you **may bring** a companion with you.

We use *might* + bare infinitive
• to talk about possibility in the future.
Helen **might go** camping with her boyfriend this weekend.
We **might** not **go** out tomorrow.
• as the past tense of *may*.
Mum said that she **might drive** me to the match tomorrow.

Unit 9

Must

We use *must* + bare infinitive to
- say that something is necessary.

*A crash helmet **must be** worn at all times.*
- talk about obligations.

*I **must get** this essay finished by tomorrow morning.*
- show that we are sure that something is true.

*Greta **must be** an athlete – look at her run!*
- recommend something.

*You **must listen** to their latest CD – it's brilliant.*

We use *mustn't* + bare infinitive to talk about something that is not allowed.
*You **mustn't smoke** in here.*

Should

We use *should* + bare infinitive to
- give advice.

*You **should get** some rest.*
- ask for advice.

***Should** I **buy** a racing bike or a mountain bike?*

Note

Ought to can also be used to give advice, but it is not usually used in the question form.

*Gina **ought to pay** her employees more.*

Would

We use *would* + bare infinitive for
- actions that we did regularly in the past, but that we don't do now.

*We **would play** tennis in the park every weekend – now we just play on our computers.*
- polite requests

***Would** you **get** me a coffee, please?*

Note

We can also use *need* as an ordinary verb. It has affirmative, negative and question forms and it is usually used in the Present Simple and the Past Simple. It is followed by a full infinitive.

*They **need to behave** better in class.*
*I **don't need to buy** a new camera – my dad knows how to fix this one.*
***Do** I **need to tell** you everything I do?*

Needn't

We use *needn't* + bare infinitive to say that something is not necessary.
*You **needn't hand in** your homework until next Friday.*

Be Able To

We use *be able to* to talk about
- general ability.

*Fortunately, we **are** now **able to apply** for a place online.*
- a specific ability in the past. (*Could* cannot be used here.)

*He **was able to escape** from the burning car.*

Have To

We use *have to* to
- say that something is necessary.

*You **have to take** great care when working with electricity.*
- talk about obligation.

*Robert **has to report** any technical problems to his manager.*

Mustn't & Don't Have To

There is an important difference between *mustn't* and *don't have to*. We use *mustn't* to say that something is not allowed, whereas we use *don't have to* to show that there is no obligation or necessity.
*Students **mustn't cut and paste** from Wikipedia when doing this project.*
*We **don't have to be** home until midnight tonight.*

Grammar Exercises

2 Circle the correct words.

1 Fortunately, we **can / were able to** reach the airport in time for our flight yesterday.
2 **Can I / Am I able to** have some more chocolate, please?
3 Although I tried hard, I **could / couldn't** beat the club champion.
4 I'd like to **can / be able to** choose my own working hours.
5 **Can you / Could you** hear the teacher clearly this morning?
6 Both his sisters **can / were able to** play a reasonably good game of chess at the age of five.
7 We **can / could** see most of the city from our old house on the top of the hill.
8 Yes, you **can / could** borrow my dress at the weekend.
9 He **can't / wasn't able to** persuade his parents to let him go on holiday with his friends last summer.
10 Sally **couldn't / won't be able to** come to lunch tomorrow; she's working.

3 Rewrite the sentences using may or might (not).

1 It is possible that she is coming home, but I am not sure.
   She _____.
2 Perhaps she is much older than she says.
   She _____.
3 Perhaps he is studying in his room.
   He _____.
4 It is possible that he will not pass his exams.
   He _____.
5 It is possible that the Browns are moving house, but I am not sure.
   The Browns _____.
6 Perhaps Jonathan is not at the meeting.
   Jonathan _____.

4 Read the sentences and then write your advice using should / ought to or shouldn't.

1 I always hurt myself when I jump down the stairs.
   You shouldn't jump down the stairs!
2 Stephan doesn't practise the piano very much.
   _____
3 My head hurts and I have got a fever.
   _____
4 I can't close this suitcase because there are too many clothes in it.
   _____
5 Eating ice cream really hurts my teeth.
   _____
6 Pamela really wants to buy a pet.
   _____
7 I get upset when I don't get 100% in a test.
   _____

Unit 9

5 Complete the sentences with must / mustn't or don't/doesn't have to.

1 You _____ come with me if you don't want to.
2 Everyone _____ obey the law.
3 He _____ rush. He's got plenty of time.
4 Peter _____ write to his friend, John, as he is seeing him next weekend.
5 Children _____ touch electrical wires.
6 You _____ play your music quietly, or you will wake the baby.
7 I _____ go to bed early tonight – there's no school tomorrow!
8 Drivers _____ throw litter out of car windows.

6 Rewrite the sentences using can't or must.

1 I am sure Susan isn't at work now. She left the office an hour ago.
Susan _____.
2 I am sure my sister is talking on the phone now. The line is busy.
My sister _____.
3 I think my mother is on her way home. She isn't answering the phone at work.
My mother _____.
4 I am sure that your son isn't doing his homework in his room. I saw him in the garden.
Your son _____.
5 I am sure she doesn't spend much money. She is poor.
She _____.
6 I am sure she is at the office now. I just spoke to her on the phone.
She _____.
7 I am sure my mother isn't cooking again. I saw her cooking at noon.
My mother _____.
8 I am sure Wendy is in Rome by now. She got on the plane hours ago.
Wendy _____.
9 I think my teacher exercises everyday. He's very fit.
My teacher _____.
10 I am sure Mary doesn't study for three hours a day. She isn't a good student.
Mary _____.

7 Complete the second sentence so that it has a similar meaning to the first sentence. Use the word in bold.

1 It isn't necessary for her to finish the report today.
have
She _____ the report today.
2 I am sure Molly is at the dentist's.
be
Molly _____ the dentist's.
3 I am sure this isn't the place we are looking for.
be
This _____ we are looking for.
4 It is possible that we will win the game.
might
We _____ the game.
5 Your doctor advises you to stop smoking.
ought
You _____ smoking.
6 Sheila managed to finish her report in one day.
was
Sheila _____ her report in one day.
7 It was not necessary for you to buy a present for me.
have
You _____ a present for me.

Vocabulary

Phrasal verbs

8 Match the phrasal verbs with their meanings.

1. hack into
2. hook up to
3. shut down
4. plug in
5. set off
6. switch on
7. break down
8. back up

a to turn on a computer, light, etc
b to make a spare copy of something on a computer
c to illegally enter another computer system
d to make an alarm ring
e to connect one machine to another
f to turn off a computer
g to suddenly stop working
h to connect a machine to an electricity supply

9 Complete the sentences with the correct form of the phrasal verbs from 8.

1. Martin was arrested for _____ the United States military computer system.
2. My laptop _____ last week and I can't afford to get it repaired.
3. It's too dark in here. Can you _____ the light, please?
4. We simply _____ the computer to the new printer, and everything worked straight away!
5. I felt silly when I realised that the computer which I thought was broken was simply not _____.
6. The alarm was _____ when a bird flew in through the front door.
7. It was past midnight when I finally _____ my computer and went to bed.
8. Always _____ your work, because you might lose it forever if you don't.

Prepositions

10 Circle the correct words.

1. Paris, **along / past / over** with Madrid and Rome, is one of the most beautiful cities in Europe.
2. Don't eat that ham! It's a week **along / past / over** its sell-by date.
3. When we realised our mistake, we had to start all **along / past / over** again.
4. I spoke to her **along / past / over** the phone last night.
5. Eventually, we did what I had been saying we should do all **along / past / over**.
6. Samantha is now **along / past / over** the age when she needs to have a babysitter.

Collocations & Expressions

11 Complete the sentences with these words. Use each word once.

answering   cash   sewing   time   vending   washing

1. I am wearing the same clothes again because our _____ machine is broken.
2. If I had a _____ machine, I'd go back to the age of the dinosaurs.
3. Is there a _____ machine near here? I need a drink.
4. Tom took £50 out of the _____ machine, and spent it all on computer games.
5. Have you got a _____ machine? My jeans need to be repaired.
6. I hate talking to _____ machines. I usually just hang up the phone without saying anything.

Unit 9

Words easily confused

12 Use the words given to complete the sentences underneath. Make sure the words are in the correct form. Use each word at least once.

1 | bring   carry   fetch   take |
   a   I think I'll _____ the children on a picnic tomorrow.
   b   We ordered fish and you've _____ us lamb.
   c   Could someone help me _____ my luggage – it's really heavy!
   d   There's a first-aid kit in the car. Please _____ it for me.

2 | avoid   ban   block   forbid   prevent |
   a   This device _____ the engine from overheating.
   b   How can I _____ speaking to her when we work in the same office?
   c   They've been _____ from the club for fighting.
   d   Taking photographs in this area is strictly _____.
   e   The defender _____ the shot and saved his team from defeat.

3 | cause   happen   lead   result |
   a   What _____ to your car?
   b   You've already _____ enough trouble, so stop it!
   c   The heavy rain _____ in floods.
   d   It was your attitude towards Jack that _____ to his decision to resign.

4 | expand   extend   increase   rise |
   a   Several shopkeepers have _____ their prices.
   b   His land _____ well beyond the river.
   c   They're thinking of _____ their business.
   d   If the temperature _____ any higher, turn on the air conditioning.
   e   Gases _____ when heated.

Word formation mixed

13 Use the word in capitals to form a word that fits in the gap.

1   This motorbike has a very _____ engine.   **POWER**
2   The boy who saved me won a medal for _____.   **BRAVE**
3   He is so _____ that he has no friends at all.   **LIKE**
4   It's a good idea to take your young dog out, so that it can _____ with other dogs.   **SOCIAL**
5   The _____ is planning to increase taxes again.   **GOVERN**
6   The two companies formed a _____, and became internationally successful.   **PARTNER**
7   I'm so _____ – I have never won anything in my life.   **LUCK**
8   That was an _____ thing to do!   **AMAZE**

Sentence transformation

14 Complete the second sentence so that it has a similar meaning to the first sentence, using the word given. Do not change the word given. You must use between two and five words.

1 I'm sure that Simon isn't 19 years old.
   be
   Simon _____ 19 years old.

2 I advise you to go and see this film.
   ought
   You _____ and see this film.

3 It wasn't necessary for them to prepare a meal for us.
   have
   They _____ prepare a meal for us.

4 You need to connect the computer to the scanner.
   hook
   You need to _____ to the computer.

5 I have a spare phone in case this one stops working.
   breaks
   If this phone _____, I'll use my spare one.

6 Always make a copy of your files.
   back
   Always _____ your files.

7 This sandwich should have been sold days ago.
   past
   This sandwich _____ date.

8 We had to go right back to the very beginning.
   all
   We had to _____ again.

Unit 10

Awareness

1 Which of these sentences are correct (C) and incorrect (I)?

1. Tom might taken your coat by mistake. ___
2. You should have been practised more. ___
3. I could have been a great footballer. ___
4. He can't have driving home last night – he doesn't have a car. ___
5. That must have been a very exciting race. ___
6. I would lent it to you if you had asked. ___
7. We needn't have hurried because the show started late. ___
8. Sorry, should I asked permission first? ___
9. Would you have gone if you had been invited? ___
10. He shouldn't have been said that to her. ___

How many did you get right? ☐

Grammar

May/Might Have

We use *may/might have* + past participle to show that we are not sure about something in the past.
Dana **may have forgotten** what time the meeting was.

Should Have

We use *should have* + past participle
• to show that something we were expecting did not happen.
Maria **should have phoned** by now.
• to criticise our own or someone else's behaviour.
You **shouldn't have tried** to fix the washing machine yourself!

Could Have

We use *could have* + past participle to
• show that we are not sure about something in the past.
I **could have made** a big mistake in that last exam.
• say that something was possible in the past, but that it didn't happen.
She **could have been** an Olympic gymnast if she hadn't been in that terrible car crash.

Can't/Couldn't Have

We use *can't/couldn't have* + past participle to show that we are sure that something is not true about the past.
Sally **can't have cooked** dinner – she has never cooked anything in her life!

Must Have

We use *must have* + past participle to show that we are sure that something is true about the past.
You **must have been** very proud when you won that prize.

Would Have

We use *would have* + past participle to say that we were willing to do something, but that we didn't do it.
I **would have bought** you that game if it had been cheaper.

Needn't Have

We use *needn't have* + past participle to say it wasn't necessary to do something, but you did it anyway.
You **needn't have bought** a new pen – this one is working fine.

Grammar Exercises

2 Use the prompts to write sentences.

1 might / arrived / She / not / yet / have
_____

2 out / gone / have / My parents / may
_____

3 wanted / to come / Simon / not / have / might
_____

4 listening / might / been / have / I / to music
_____

5 have / not / The students / about it / might / known / anything
_____

6 a lot of / been / have / people / There / at the theatre / may
_____

7 well / Daniel / last night / been / not / might / feeling / have
_____

8 your / may / You / broken / finger / have
_____

3 Complete the sentences with can't have or must have and the past participle of the verbs in brackets.

1 **A:** Did they go to the cinema yesterday?
   B: They _____ (go) because there was no one at home when I called.
2 Kate is exhausted. She _____ (work) hard in the garden today.
3 Susan's telephone was out of order yesterday. She _____ (phone) you.
4 She hadn't seen him before, so she _____ (recognise) him.
5 I called her twice, but she didn't answer the phone. She _____ (be) asleep.
6 **A:** John translated the letter for me.
   B: John doesn't speak French, so he _____ (translate) it.
7 Emma has been at home all day. You _____ (see) her at the restaurant.
8 She asked me for money again. She _____ (spend) all the money I gave her.

4 Rewrite the sentences using should have / shouldn't have.

1 Tom was supposed to be sleeping.
   Tom _____.
2 Jim was supposed to bring all the documents.
   Jim _____.
3 My brother didn't buy any food for the party.
   My brother _____.
4 He didn't arrive on time for the rehearsal.
   He _____.
5 Ben lied to his parents.
   Ben _____.
6 My brother didn't mention the accident.
   My brother _____.

Unit 10

5 Rewrite the sentences using **needn't have** or **didn't have to**.

1. It was unnecessary for you to bring all this food. You're very kind.
   You _____.
2. It wasn't necessary for me to get up early this morning; that's why I slept till late.
   I _____.
3. I didn't go shopping today. I went yesterday.
   I _____.
4. She watered the flowers this morning, but it rained later.
   She _____.
5. My mother didn't cook today. We had booked a restaurant.
   My mother _____.
6. I studied for the test, but it was incredibly easy.
   I _____.

6 Complete the second sentence so that it has a similar meaning to the first sentence. Use the word in bold.

1. Perhaps your son took your car.
   have
   Your son _____ your car.
2. I'm sure that you didn't see Mary in the city centre.
   seen
   You _____ Mary in the city centre.
3. I am sure my mother cooked this delicious meal.
   must
   My mother _____ this delicious meal.
4. Thank you very much for the sweets. It wasn't necessary.
   brought
   You _____ sweets with you.
5. You didn't ask your parents first.
   asked
   You _____ first.
6. Perhaps he left his car keys at home.
   may
   He _____ car keys at home.
7. I am sure he was eating when I called.
   been
   He _____ when I called.
8. It was too big, so I didn't buy it.
   bought
   I _____ if it had been smaller.

Vocabulary

Phrasal verbs

7 Match the phrasal verbs with their meanings.

1. log in ☐   a to happen in a way that was not expected
2. log out ☐   b to return the way you came from
3. key in ☐   c to join a computer network
4. turn out ☐   d to make the volume or heat lower
5. turn up ☐   e to ask someone for help or support
6. turn down ☐   f to make the volume or heat higher
7. turn to ☐   g to type something into a computer
8. turn back ☐   h to disconnect from a computer network

8 Complete the sentences with the correct form of the phrasal verbs from 7.
1 I can't _____ to this account without a password.
2 When I have trouble with my homework, I always _____ my older sister for help.
3 Can you _____ your music, please? I'm trying to work.
4 We didn't know why our computer was acting strangely. It _____ that it had a virus.
5 The weather was so bad that we had to _____ and go home.
6 _____ the heating. It's freezing in here!
7 Always remember to _____ from your email account when you are using a public computer.
8 Could you _____ this data for me, please?

Prepositions

9 Circle the correct words.
1 I don't know what's wrong **with / within / without** this printer!
2 Our service engineer will call you **with / within / without** the next few days.
3 Please respond to this letter **with / within / without** delay.
4 We managed to keep our spending **with / within / without** budget on our last holiday.
5 It's really hard to work **with / within / without** all that noise going on next door.
6 She worked continuously from 9 am until 9 pm **with / within / without** taking a break.

Collocations & Expressions

10 Complete the sentences with these words.

| attention   business   consideration   control   convenience   difference |

1 When you mark my exam, please take into _____ the fact that I was ill.
2 I have left my essay on your desk for you to read at your _____.
3 It makes no _____ what food I give it, the cat refuses to eat anything.
4 I'm sorry, but what happens from now on is beyond my _____.
5 It's none of your _____ how much money my father earns!
6 Try to catch the waiter's _____ – I want to ask for the bill.

Words easily confused

11 Use the words given to complete the sentences underneath. Make sure the words are in the correct form. Use each word at least once.

1 | arrive   get   reach |
   a She _____ at the party in a satin dress.
   b After an hour's walk, we _____ to the bridge.
   c The plane is due to _____ the airport in 20 minutes.

2 | angle   corner   edge   margin   view |
   a Leave the bag in the _____ next to the lamp.
   b Let's look at the problem from a different _____.
   c Why does your point of _____ always differ from mine?
   d Don't write in the _____ because that's where the teacher makes her comments.
   e They stood at the water's _____ and gazed at the sunset.

3 | certainly   likely   possibly   probably |
   a Don't worry. They're _____ on their way here.
   b It's _____ that Johnson will win the race.
   c I'm _____ not going to lend him any more CDs! He never returns them.
   d I could be wrong, but that's _____ the worst song I've ever heard.

Unit 10 71

Unit 10

Word formation mixed

12 Use the word in capitals to form a word that fits in the gap.

1. All of the _____ in the play were professional actors. **PERFORM**
2. That's the _____ camera I have ever seen. **TINY**
3. I _____ spilled coffee all over my keyboard. **ACCIDENT**
4. I _____ believe that Mark and Julie will be very happy together. **TRUE**
5. We spent a _____ afternoon without the children. **PEACE**
6. The _____ in this part of the country is amazing. **SCENE**
7. Thank you. Your _____ is really appreciated. **KIND**
8. He was lucky to be _____ after a fall like that! **LIVE**

Sentence transformation

13 Complete the second sentence so that it has a similar meaning to the first sentence, using the word given. Do not change the word given. You must use between two and five words.

1. It was a bad idea to eat that old ham.
   eaten
   You _____ that old ham.

2. I wasn't invited to the party, so I didn't go.
   would
   I _____ to the party if I had been invited.

3. I am certain she was sleeping when I phoned her.
   been
   She _____ when I phoned her.

4. I thought it was a letter, but it was actually a bill.
   out
   What I thought was a letter _____ a bill.

5. Please do not wait before paying this bill.
   without
   Pay this bill _____, please.

6. She won't forgive you no matter what you say.
   difference
   It _____ what you say, she won't forgive you.

7. I was trying to make her notice me, so that I could ask her name.
   catch
   I was trying _____, so that I could ask her name.

8. You have no right to know about my private life, so don't ask me about it.
   none
   My private life _____, so don't ask me about it.

Unit 11

Awareness

1 Which of these sentences are correct (C) and incorrect (I)?

1. Have you finished tidy your room? ___
2. Your bungalow will be cleaned daily. ___
3. I'm pleased to hear that you have recovered. ___
4. She persuaded him buying her a diamond necklace. ___
5. It's not worth to worry about it. ___
6. We weren't allowed take mobile phones with us. ___
7. The teacher made me write the essay again. ___
8. I wasn't expecting meet anyone I knew. ___
9. Steve had difficulty understanding the documents. ___
10. Do you remember visiting this place for the first time? ___

How many did you get right? ☐

Grammar

Gerunds

We form gerunds with verbs and the *-ing* ending. We can use gerunds
• as nouns.
Smoking is very bad for you.
• after prepositions.
I'm excited **about coming** to see you.
• after the verb *go* when we talk about activities.
Terry **goes skiing** every winter.

We also use gerunds after certain verbs and phrases.
admit, finish, love, avoid, forgive, miss, be used to, hate, practise, can't help, have difficulty, prefer, can't stand, imagine, prevent, deny, involve, regret, dislike, it's no good, risk, (don't) mind, it's no use, spend time, enjoy, it's (not) worth, suggest, fancy, keep, feel like, like
I don't feel like cooking tonight.
It's not worth paying someone to repair this old car.

Infinitives

	Active	Passive
Present	(to) make	(to) be made
Perfect	(to) have made	(to) have been made

We will **fix** your TV.
Our TV will **be fixed**.
They shouldn't **have sold** their house.
Their house shouldn't **have been sold**.

Full Infinitives

We form full infinitives with *to* and the verb. We use full infinitives
• to explain purpose.
I went into town **to inquire** about night classes.
• after adjectives such as *afraid, scared, happy, glad, pleased, sad,* etc.
My father was **happy to hear** I had passed all my exams.
• after the words *too* and *enough*.
You're **too** young **to watch** this film.
You aren't old **enough to watch** this film.

We also use full infinitives after certain verbs and phrases.
afford, fail, prepare, agree, forget, pretend, allow, hope, promise, appear, invite, refuse, arrange, learn, seem, ask, manage, start, begin, need, want, choose, offer, would like, decide, persuade, expect, plan
Graham and Martin **decided to work** on the project together.
Would you **like to come** bowling with us?

Unit 11

Bare Infinitives

We use bare infinitives after
• modal verbs.
You **can help** me with this if you want.
• *had better* to give advice.
We **had better run** or we'll miss the train.
• *would rather* to talk about preference. We often use the word *than*.
I **would rather go** to the beach **than** the park.

We use *make* + object + bare infinitive when we want to say that we force a person to do something in the active voice, but in the passive it's followed by a full infinitive.
My mother **made** me **tidy** my room again.
I **was made to tidy** my room again by my mother.

> **Note**
>
> We use *let* + object + bare infinitive when we want to say that we give permission for someone to do something and it is only used in the active voice. In the passive we can use the verb *to be allowed to*.
>
> The teacher **let** us **take** a five-minute break at ten o'clock.
> We **were allowed to take** a five-minute break at ten o'clock.

Gerund or Infinitive?

Some verbs can be followed by a gerund or a full infinitive with no change in meaning. Some common verbs are *begin, bother, continue, hate, like, love* and *start*.
The baby began **crying/to cry** when the dog barked.
I hated **doing/to do** jigsaw puzzles when I was a child.
Don't bother **trying/to try** getting tickets for the concert.

There are other verbs that can be followed by a gerund or a full infinitive, but the meaning changes. Some common ones are *go on, forget, regret, remember, stop* and *try*.
I **forgot buying** that book. (I didn't remember that I had bought that book.)
I **forgot to buy** the book. (I didn't remember to buy the book, so I don't have it.)
We **went on running** through the rain. (They continued to run.)
We **went on to run** to the top of Box Hill. (They had been running for a while, then continued running to the top of the hill.)
I **regret not asking** Kim to dance. (I didn't ask Kim to dance, but now I regret it.)
We **regret to inform** you that the basketball match has been cancelled. (We're sorry that we have to tell you this.)
My dad **remembers seeing** U2 perform at Wembley. (He saw U2 and now he remembers seeing them.)
I **remembered to take** my library books back today. (I remembered first and then I took the books back.)
We **stopped revising** because it was late. (We didn't revise any more.)
We **stopped to have** a cup of coffee. (We stopped doing something, so we could have a cup of coffee.)
Try turning the computer off and then on again. (Do it and see if that works.)
I **tried to turn** the computer off, but didn't know how. (I made the effort, but didn't succeed.)

Grammar Exercises

2 Circle the correct words.

1. It's no use **talking / to talk** to Mary; she won't listen to you.
2. You were so lucky **escape / to have escaped** from the building during the earthquake.
3. It was so kind of you **to take / taking** me to hospital.
4. Could you **get / to get** tickets for the science fair?
5. The suspect denied **knowing / to know** anything about it.
6. Samantha couldn't afford **going / to go** on holiday this year.
7. You had better **to hurry / hurry**, or else you will miss the train.
8. Carol avoided **driving / to drive** in the rush hour when she lived in Paris.
9. My parents don't let me **staying / stay** up late during the week.
10. My secretary reminded me **replying / to reply** to a letter.

3 Use the prompts to write sentences.

1 I / not remember / get / a letter from you

2 it / be / very kind / you / send / me / flowers / yesterday

3 they / tried / prevent me from / appear in court / but I finally / manage / do it

4 they / accuse him of / steal / the money and he admitted / do it in the end

5 it / take / her / ages / get / over / her illness / last year

6 there / be / no point in / complain about / spend / so much money on the car

7 he / be / the only student / pass / the exam

8 my brother / spend / most of his free time / listen to music and / watch TV

9 it / be / cruel / him / hit / his dog

10 it / be / impossible / me / meet / you right now

4 Complete the sentences with the gerund or infinitive form of the verbs in brackets.

1 Do you feel like _____ (go) out or would you rather _____ (stay) in tonight?
2 Did they manage _____ (carry) the new bed upstairs?
3 I always enjoy _____ (eat) out with friends.
4 I'd like _____ (eat) in a Chinese restaurant for a change.
5 A: Did you remember _____ (lock) the door?
   B: No, I didn't. I'd better _____ (go) back and _____ (do) it now.
6 She remembers _____ (go) to school for the first time.
7 After _____ (spend) two weeks alone, she looked forward to _____ (see) us all.
8 She was the only one _____ (arrive) at the meeting on time.
9 She pretended _____ (be) sick in order to avoid _____ (go) to school.
10 My parents think that I am incapable of _____ (earn) a living.

Unit 11

5 Rewrite the sentences using these verbs.

> accuse   admit   agree   apologise   deny   promise   refuse   suggest

1. My sister said, 'No, I didn't take your car.'
   My sister denied taking my car.
2. Ann said to me, 'No, I won't give you any money.'
   Ann _____ me any money.
3. Bill said to his wife, 'I am so sorry I spoilt our holiday.'
   Bill _____ their holiday.
4. Martha said, 'Let's go sailing this weekend.'
   Martha _____ sailing that weekend.
5. Alice said to me, 'Yes, I'll help you with your homework.'
   Alice _____ me with my homework.
6. Brenda said to me, 'You took my watch.'
   Brenda _____ her watch.
7. The man said, 'Yes, I stole the car.'
   The man _____ the car.
8. 'Don't worry, Peter; I'll take you to the park tomorrow,' said his father.
   Peter's father _____ him to the park the next day.

6 Find the mistakes and correct the sentences where necessary. Put a tick (✓) below those which do not need correcting.

1. She couldn't cope with worked for so many hours a day.
   _____
2. Pam would rather to drink wine than beer.
   _____
3. She admitted to steal the money from the safe.
   _____
4. Mr Anderson can't stand to be treated dishonestly.
   _____
5. They postponed going to see their grandparents.
   _____
6. I don't remember arranging a meeting for today.
   _____
7. Jim advised me working overtime to earn more money.
   _____
8. I don't enjoy to be in crowded places.
   _____

7 Complete the sentences about you.

1. I really can't afford _____.
2. I spend my spare time _____.
3. My parents don't let me _____.
4. I am old enough _____.
5. I really can't stand _____.
6. I avoid _____.
7. It's dangerous _____.
8. I promised _____.

Vocabulary

Phrasal verbs

8 Match the phrasal verbs with their meanings.

1. feel up to
2. get together
3. get away with
4. run into
5. run over
6. run away
7. show up
8. show around

a. to meet with socially
b. to leave a place secretly
c. to escape punishment for doing something wrong
d. to show someone a place
e. to meet someone by chance
f. to arrive somewhere, usually unexpectedly
g. to be well or confident enough to do something
h. to hit someone with a vehicle

9 Complete the sentences with the correct form of the phrasal verbs from 8.

1. Let's stay at home tonight. I still don't _____ going out.
2. Every year the old school friends _____ for a meal.
3. Ivan was a new student, so I volunteered to _____ him _____ on his first day.
4. Did you really think you could _____ copying your whole project from the Internet?
5. Daniella _____ from home at the age of 17, but she came back two days later.
6. Our cat has been _____ by a car twice, but he's still okay!
7. I _____ my old English teacher at the supermarket yesterday.
8. We waited for half an hour for Simon to _____, but he never did.

Prepositions

10 Circle the correct words.

1. **On / In / At** second thoughts, I'd rather go to the tennis match tomorrow.
2. I'm **on / in / at** two minds about whether or not to go rock climbing this weekend.
3. If you're **on / in / at** a loose end, why not come round to my house and play computer games?
4. She wants **on / in / at** least £100 for her old bicycle, but I don't think it's worth it.
5. He only ever visits his grandmother once **on / in / at** a blue moon.
6. It was raining, I was hungry and **on / in / at** top of all that, I had a cold.

Collocations & Expressions

11 Complete the sentences with the correct form of **play**, **do** or **go**.

1. How often do you _____ climbing?
2. My aunt _____ yoga three times a week.
3. The only sport I enjoy _____ is volleyball.
4. Gary has been _____ karate for five years, and now he has a black belt.
5. Do you want to _____ bungee jumping with me next week?
6. I've _____ chess since I was eight years old, but I'm still not very good at it.

Unit 11

Words easily confused

12 Use the words given to complete the sentences underneath. Make sure the words are in the correct form. Use each word at least once.

1 **discover find out invent set up**
   a It was Henri Becquerel who _____ radioactivity.
   b Can you _____ when the bus leaves, please?
   c One type of telescope was _____ by Sir William Herschel.
   d His grandfather _____ the company 60 years ago.

2 **logical reasonable sensible sensitive**
   a She wears sunglasses because her eyes are _____ to light.
   b He's so _____ that he gets upset when you criticise him.
   c Being so _____, Julie is in great demand as a babysitter.
   d I tried to be _____, but they refused to cooperate.
   e There's no _____ explanation for this event.

3 **abandon desert disappear mislay**
   a The weather was so bad that the navy had to _____ the search for the missing sailors.
   b The soldier _____ his post during the battle.
   c As the fog descended, the block of flats opposite slowly _____ from view.
   d I seem to have _____ my pen. Have you seen it?

4 **accurate exact precise**
   a This watch is _____ to within five seconds a decade.
   b I had the printer make a(n) _____ copy of an old poster which had been torn.
   c You said you left at about midnight. Can you try to be more _____, please?

Word formation mixed

13 Use the word in capitals to form a word that fits in the gap.

1 The children should be congratulated for putting on such a _____ performance. **MEMORY**
2 Before you go to university, you need to decide what subject you want to _____ in. **SPECIAL**
3 There is a _____ looking man hanging around outside the library. **SUSPECT**
4 Symptoms of the disease include headaches, fever, and a constant feeling of _____. **WEAK**
5 The boys watched in _____ as the stunt rider performed his tricks. **AMAZE**
6 This club has a large _____, consisting of people of all ages. **MEMBER**
7 My parents have been _____ married for 45 years. **HAPPY**
8 I don't just _____ boxing, I hate it. **LIKE**

Sentence transformation

14 Complete the second sentence so that it has a similar meaning to the first sentence, using the word given. Do not change the word given. You must use between two and five words.

1 'You'd better stay in bed for a couple of days,' said the doctor.
   advised
   The doctor _____ in bed for a couple of days.

2 Driving without a licence is illegal.
   to
   It's _____ a licence.

3 I'd buy this house, but I don't have enough money.
   afford
   I _____ this house.

4 Jenny's mother thinks Jenny must tidy her room.
   wants
   Jenny's mother _____ her room.

5 Perhaps James wasn't telling the truth.
   been
   James _____ the truth.

6 We very rarely have pizza for dinner.
   moon
   Once _____ we have pizza for dinner.

7 You will be punished for cheating in the test.
   away
   You _____ cheating in the test.

8 I unexpectedly met Ian when I was in London.
   ran
   When I was in London, _____ Ian.

Unit 12

Awareness

1 Which of these sentences are correct (C) and incorrect (I)?

1. I'd like to know when you are arriving. ___
2. You aren't very helpful, aren't you? ___
3. Wasn't that a great match? ___
4. Why you didn't tell me about this? ___
5. Could you to give me directions to the bank? ___
6. Let's go to the beach, shall we? ___
7. Don't talk so quickly, do you? ___
8. Doesn't she look lovely in that dress? ___
9. I'm very late, aren't I? ___
10. Do you know if Jane is coming to the meeting? ___

How many did you get right? ☐

Grammar

Indirect Questions

You can introduce a question indirectly by using indirect question forms. For indirect questions, we use the word order of a normal statement and we sometimes end them with a full stop instead of a question mark. Indirect questions are considered to be more polite than direct questions.
I'd like to know when the exam begins.
Could you give me a hand with this luggage?

Questions for which the answer is *yes* or *no* require the word *if* or *whether*.
*Do you know **if** Marco is coming to school today?*
*Could you tell me **whether** there is a post office near here?*

Question Tags

Question tags are short questions at the end of a positive or negative sentence. They are formed with a modal or an auxiliary verb + a personal pronoun.
We usually use an affirmative question tag after a negative sentence, and a negative question tag after an affirmative sentence.
*She has been all over the world, **hasn't she**?*
*You can't solve this puzzle, **can you**?*

When an affirmative sentence contains a verb in the Present Simple or the Past Simple we use *do/does*, *don't/doesn't* and *did/didn't* in the question tag.
*Ben loves windsurfing, **doesn't he**?*
*They had a good time last night, **didn't they**?*

We use question tags when we want
• someone to agree with what we are saying.
*That was a delicious meal, **wasn't it**?*
• to make sure that what we are saying is right.
*We go to the same school, **don't we**?*

Remember! Some question tags are irregular. Notice the way these tags are formed.
***I am** a good student, **aren't I**?*
***Everyone is** happy, **aren't they**?*
***Let's** do this tomorrow, **shall we**?*
***Don't** drive so fast, **will you**?*
***Take** good **care** of yourself, **won't you**?*
***This/That is** amazing, **isn't it**?*
***These/Those are** wonderful paintings, **aren't they**?*

Negative Questions

Negative questions can be used
- in exclamations.

*Wow! **Wasn't** that an interesting lesson!*
- to show that we are surprised or doubtful.

***Haven't** you seen that film yet?*
*Why **didn't** he phone me when he had the chance?*
- when we expect someone to agree with us.

***Doesn't** Sarah's new hairstyle look great?*

Grammar Exercises

2 Circle the correct words.

1. I'd **wonder / like** to know where you bought that hat.
2. **Would / Could** you mind telling me where the exit is?
3. I don't **mind / suppose** you know how to get to the station from here.
4. Do you know **what / if** the post has been delivered yet?
5. I **suppose / wonder** if she would like to come to the art gallery.
6. **Do / Could** you tell me whether it's going to rain today?
7. I **could / would** like to ask you why this is so expensive.

3 Complete the indirect questions.

1. Where is the bathroom?
   Could you tell me _____?
2. How much does this cost?
   I wonder if you know _____.
3. When do the tickets go on sale?
   I don't suppose you know _____.
4. Do you want to take a short break?
   I wonder _____.
5. Is that St Paul's Cathedral over there?
   Do you know _____?
6. Did the children enjoy the show?
   I'd like to ask you _____.
7. What's the time?
   Would you mind _____?

4 Match the sentences with the question tags.

1. You paid the rent on Monday,   a won't they?
2. There aren't any vacancies at the factory,   b does it?
3. Let's turn off the television,   c aren't I?
4. They never get travel sick,   d has she?
5. They'll be here soon,   e didn't you?
6. She's never beaten you at tennis,   f shall we?
7. It doesn't hurt,   g are there?
8. I am right,   h do they?

Unit 12 81

Unit 12

5 Add question tags to these sentences.
1 I'd better leave, _____?
2 Patrick can't drive, _____?
3 There weren't many people in the restaurant, _____?
4 He broke the world record last year, _____?
5 I'm improving, _____?
6 Help me with this assignment, _____?
7 Let's go swimming, _____?
8 Those are your neighbours, _____?

6 Complete the negative questions.
1 _____ you surprised that they won the championship?
2 _____ the weather been terrible recently?
3 _____ that the most amazing view you have ever seen?
4 Why _____ Martha home until after midnight?
5 _____ it be great if Dad bought a new sports car?
6 _____ you heard the news about the president?
7 _____ they happy to be sent home early from school yesterday?
8 _____ it a lovely day!

7 Complete the sentences with the word that best fits each gap.
1 Do you know _____ Simon is at home?
2 They don't enjoy visiting me in hospital, _____ they?
3 _____ didn't she phone a taxi?
4 I'd _____ to know where you got those tickets.
5 Let's go home, _____ we?
6 Everyone loves chocolate, don't _____?

Vocabulary

Phrasal verbs

8 Match the phrasal verbs with their meanings.
1 sit around
2 sit back
3 pass around
4 stand back
5 sleep in
6 believe in
7 turn down
8 cut down

a to get out of bed later than usual
b to stay at home being lazy
c to rest comfortably on a chair or sofa
d to reject an invitation
e to offer something to each person in a group
f to move a short distance from something
g to be sure that something is right
h to reduce the amount of something

9 Complete the sentences with the correct form of the phrasal verbs from 8.
1 The doctor advised my uncle to _____ the amount of chocolate he eats.
2 I _____ my place at a university in London because I wanted to live near my parents.
3 She gets very bored just _____ the house all day, doing nothing.
4 Sorry I'm late. I _____ this morning because my alarm didn't go off!
5 He _____ in his chair, picked up his book, and began to read.
6 Why don't you _____ that bottle of water, so that everyone can have a drink?
7 Steve _____ always being honest with people, even if they might be offended.
8 You should _____ from the edge of the bicycle track or you might get hit.

Prepositions

10 Circle the correct words.

1 With the recent change of government, the economic situation has just gone **for / from / with** bad to worse.
2 We can't afford another car, so this one will just have to do **for / from / with** the moment.
3 Why don't you want to come to the beach? What's wrong **for / from / with** you?
4 Is this just a rehearsal or is it **for / from / with** real?
5 Tony was promoted **for / from / with** shop assistant to manager in her first month.
6 I am writing **for / from / with** reference to our recent stay at your hotel in Monaco.

Collocations & Expressions

11 Complete the sentences with these words.

| absorbed   alone   amused   ashamed   associated   blank |

1 Leave me _____! I don't want to see anybody today.
2 You shouldn't worry about what people think of you. You've got nothing to be _____ of.
3 Our babysitter is very good at keeping the children _____ while we are out.
4 Every time I sit down to write an essay my mind goes _____.
5 He left the company because he didn't want to be _____ with the film industry anymore.
6 I'm not sure what Daniel is doing, but he is completely _____ in it. He hasn't come out of his room for hours!

Words easily confused

12 Use the words given to complete the sentences underneath. Make sure the words are in the correct form. Use each word at least once.

1 | notice   observe   see   watch |
  a The zoologist spent days _____ the behaviour of a pride of lions.
  b Can you _____ the sea from the top of the hill?
  c It's such a small stain that no one will _____ it.
  d I'd rather _____ television than go out.

2 | coast   port   resort   seaside   shore |
  a A day at the _____ would make a pleasant change.
  b Cannes is a popular tourist _____.
  c Navy vessels patrol the _____ in search of pirates.
  d Our boat sank, but we were able to swim to the _____.
  e Oil tankers are too big for this small _____.

3 | commentator   correspondent   editor   reporter |
  a A(n) _____ decides which articles are included in a newspaper.
  b He's worked as a war _____ for the last ten years.
  c At the start of the football match, the _____ predicted a win for Brazil.
  d The _____ asked the president some tricky questions at the press conference.

4 | qualification   skill   talent |
  a She has all the _____ necessary for the job.
  b On paper, the candidate had plenty of _____, but very little experience.
  c Nowadays _____ scouts watch children play football and try to sign them at a very young age.

Unit 12

Word formation mixed

13 Use the word in capitals to form a word that fits in the gap.

1 My father is a professional _____ who works for the government. **ECONOMY**
2 Sonja sat back in her chair and stared _____ out of the window. **THOUGHT**
3 If you get a reputation for _____, nobody will want to do business with you. **HONEST**
4 The police interviewed the suspect in the _____ of a lawyer. **PRESENT**
5 My _____ for a holiday destination is probably different from yours. **PREFER**
6 We haven't got an _____ supply of money, you know. **END**
7 My aunt and uncle are always arguing with each other – they seem to _____ about everything. **AGREE**
8 I can't do that because it is _____. **POSSIBLE**

Sentence transformation

14 Complete the second sentence so that it has a similar meaning to the first sentence, using the word given. Do not change the word given. You must use between two and five words.

1 Are there any tickets left?
   whether
   Could you _____ any tickets left?

2 When does the train arrive in Coventry?
   when
   I'd like to know _____ in Coventry.

3 Is there a bank near here?
   suppose
   I don't _____ a bank near here.

4 Step away from the doors, or you might fall out.
   stand
   You might fall out if you _____ from the doors.

5 She was invited to the party, but she decided not to go.
   down
   She _____ the invitation to the party.

6 You should reduce the number of cigarettes you smoke.
   cut
   You _____ the number of cigarettes you smoke.

7 Let's sit down and rest here for now.
   moment
   For _____, let's sit down and rest here.

8 I'm writing about your job advert.
   reference
   I'm writing _____ your job advert.

Review 3

B2 Practice: FCE

Part 1

For questions 1–12, read the text below and decide which answer (A, B, C or D) best fits each gap. There is an example at the beginning (0).

A new breed of superstar

Nowadays, many people become household names through professions that were once **(0)** ___ of as simply respectable, rather than glamorous. Take lawyers, for example. Getting a job with a top law **(1)** ___ may not only ensure financial security due to the astronomical **(2)** ___ lawyers can command, but it may also bring the same superstar **(3)** ___ as that of a Hollywood actor. There are very few Americans who do not **(4)** ___ the name of the independent public prosecutor, Kenneth Starr.

But a person must be **(5)** ___ out to be a lawyer in order to be successful. Firstly, a persuasive character is essential to getting every member of the jury to **(6)** ___ in with your line of argument. Secondly, the **(7)** ___ to judge character is vital, since a witness's **(8)** ___ to a question may be more significant than the answer given. **(9)** ___, leadership qualities are fundamental. Top lawyers do not have the time to **(10)** ___ all the research necessary in a case by themselves. As a **(11)** ___, they have to set an example for those under their command, so that they can **(12)** ___ on the team to work conscientiously.

0	A	looked	B	regarded	C	considered	(D)	thought
1	A	company	B	firm	C	industry	D	business
2	A	tips	B	fares	C	rewards	D	fees
3	A	level	B	fame	C	status	D	stance
4	A	recognise	B	remind	C	memorise	D	retain
5	A	suited	B	cut	C	stood	D	made
6	A	go	B	call	C	get	D	fall
7	A	certainty	B	capability	C	will	D	ability
8	A	look	B	reaction	C	action	D	response
9	A	Eventually	B	Finally	C	Ultimately	D	Conclusively
10	A	take	B	do	C	make	D	carry
11	A	end	B	result	C	score	D	sum
12	A	trust	B	believe	C	count	D	confide

Part 2

For questions 13–24, read the text below and think of the word which best fits each gap. Use only one word in each gap. There is an example at the beginning (0).

Robert Burns

Robert Burns, Scotland's greatest poet, **(0)** ___was___ born in 1759. **(13)** _____ an early age he had to help his father on his farm, as **(14)** _____ as attend school lessons.

When he was 22, he moved to Irvine, where he began to learn about making cloth. Shortly after **(15)** _____ arrival, the factory in which he was training was destroyed by fire, so he started a farm with his younger brother Gilbert.

While he was living on the farm, he concentrated **(16)** _____ writing poems and fell **(17)** _____ a local girl, Jean Armour. Robert wanted to marry her, but her father **(18)** _____ not allow him to do so. This took Robert **(19)** _____ surprise, and since he could not **(20)** _____ used to the idea of being unable to marry her, he decided to leave the country. **(21)** _____ very little money, Robert had to obtain the fare for the voyage by selling some poems. Just as he was about to leave, he **(22)** _____ advised to publish some of the poems he **(23)** _____ written. He received a large sum of money for the poetry and was then **(24)** _____ to get married to Jean.

Part 3

For questions 25–34, read the text below. Use the word given in capitals at the end of each line to form a word that fits in the gap in the same line. There is an example at the beginning (0).

Extreme sports

In the past few years, extreme sports have **(0)** ___greatly___ increased in popularity, particularly among young, well-paid professionals. But why do people take up such apparently **(25)** _____ activities? What is the attraction of doing things like bungee jumping, hang-gliding, or jumping off a cliff with a parachute? Extreme sports lovers say they get no **(26)** _____ from traditional sports or even **(27)** _____. They claim that their boring daily routine does not **(28)** _____ them to live life to the full. Only when putting their lives at risk do they feel truly alive.

Nowadays, **(29)** _____ in America, there are extreme sports competitions in which those people **(30)** _____ enough to face the challenge of these **(31)** _____ new activities can win large cash prizes. This, in turn, has increased their popularity, and has resulted in the **(32)** _____ of a whole new industry which specializes in making **(33)** _____ and clothing for extreme games. It has become a multi-million dollar business. Often the **(34)** _____ that certain games have become commercial causes other people to come up with even more extreme sports and the cycle is repeated.

GREAT
DANGER

SATISFY
ATHLETE
ABLE

SPECIAL
COURAGE
REVOLUTION

CREATE
EQUIP
DISCOVER

Part 4

For questions 35–42, complete the second sentence so that it has a similar meaning to the first sentence, using the word given. Do not change the word given. You must use between two and five words, including the word given. Here is an example (0).

Example:

0 Have you been invited to John's party?
invitation
Has John _____*sent you an invitation*_____ to his party?

35 We can be sure that Jane will help at the party.
count
We can _____ help at the party.

36 The house was completely empty.
furniture
There _____ the house.

37 I'm sure they were asleep during the burglary.
must
They _____ during the burglary.

38 My dentist advised me to reduce the amount of chocolate I ate.
advice
My _____ down on chocolate.

39 When we got to Dover, the ferry wasn't there.
already
The ferry _____ the time we got to Dover.

40 Whenever he visited us he brought flowers.
would
He _____ bringing flowers.

41 Ingrid and Astrid have had many arguments in the past.
fallen
It's not the first time Ingrid _____ Astrid.

42 You need to be courageous and determined in order to be a good soldier.
calls
Being a good soldier _____ and determination.

Review 3

Review 3

B2 Practice: ECCE

Grammar

For questions 1–20 choose the word or phrase that best completes the sentence or conversation.

1 'Nobody was there when I arrived.'
   'You might have been ___ about the start time.'
   A mistook
   B mistaken
   C mistaked
   D mistaking

2 Samantha should never ___ married that man.
   A have
   B had
   C been
   D of

3 I'd like to ___ who stole my laptop.
   A tell
   B know
   C believe
   D suppose

4 Those ships are all from the same country, ___?
   A aren't they
   B aren't those
   C they are
   D those aren't

5 'Why are you pretending ___ a bad leg?'
   'I don't want to do PE this afternoon.'
   A having
   B to have
   C have
   D to having

6 'I don't like this strange green stuff.'
   '___ you ever tasted spinach?'
   A Didn't
   B Aren't
   C Haven't
   D Weren't

7 Can you imagine ___ in a mansion?
   A living
   B to live
   C live
   D to living

8 Our car broke ___ on the way to the opera.
   A up
   B out
   C in
   D down

9 My dad made me ___ his car this morning.
   A cleaning
   B to clean
   C clean
   D to cleaning

10 It was very kind of you to help. You didn't ___.
   A should
   B might
   C have to
   D may

11 Fortunately, we ___ escape from the fire.
   A were able to
   B weren't able to
   C had to
   D wouldn't

12 'I think they missed their train.'
   'They ___ have missed the train – I left them at the station with plenty of time to spare!'
   A must
   B mustn't
   C can't
   D could

13 Let's have a game of tennis, ___?
   A have we
   B let we
   C will we
   D shall we

14 He ___ be a grandfather. He looks so young!
   A mustn't
   B needn't
   C couldn't
   D can't

15 When we were young, we ___ climb trees.
   A used
   B would
   C may
   D should

16 I prefer watching football ___ it.
   A playing
   B to play
   C play
   D to playing

17 You ___ have bothered asking, he was always going to say 'no'.
   A couldn't
   B should
   C needn't
   B didn't

18 You really ___ to study a bit harder.
   A should
   B ought
   C must
   D could

19 Toby's a careless rider, ___ ,
   A is he?
   B does he?
   C isn't he?
   D hasn't he?

20 I think she'd rather ___ out than stay home.
   A to go
   B go
   C going
   D went

Vocabulary

For questions 21–40, choose the word or phrase that most appropriately completes the sentence.

21 I'm afraid these legal proceedings are beyond my ___.
   A aim
   B influence
   C control
   D ability

22 On ___ of all that, I had a project to hand in by the next morning.
   A extra
   B side
   C bottom
   D top

23 Jo doesn't ___ up to going back to school yet.
   A feel
   B make
   C look
   D live

24 People shouldn't get ___ with throwing litter out of their car windows.
   A on
   B off
   C away
   D over

25 I'm sorry, I don't know – my mind has gone ___.
   A white
   B blank
   C empty
   D black

26 It doesn't ___ any difference how much you offer to pay him.
   A do
   B make
   C have
   D hold

27 Do you remember how to ___ in to your *Facebook* account?
   A log
   B go
   C key
   D turn

28 I left a message on your answering ___ last night.
   A box
   B phone
   C machine
   D engine

29 This situation has gone from ___ to worse.
   A bad
   B wrong
   C mistake
   D off

30 Are we playing for ___ now?
   A true
   B honest
   C real
   D fact

31 On second ___, let's just stay in and watch TV.
   A beliefs
   B thoughts
   C thinks
   D ideas

32 Why did he turn ___ the job?
   A up
   B off
   C down
   D around

33 I need to be left ___, so that I can work.
   A lonely
   B solo
   C only
   D alone

34 We missed the flight because we slept ___.
   A in
   B on
   C under
   D over

35 Don't forget to ___ some food with you on the trip.
   A fetch
   B carry
   C hold
   D bring

36 That's what I've been trying to tell you all ___!
   A along
   B over
   C past
   D across

37 Let's all get ___ for a coffee and a chat sometime this week.
   A in
   B around
   C about
   D together

38 Somebody has hacked ___ my computer and stolen my passwords.
   A over
   B on
   C into
   D off

39 Turn ___ the music. I can't hear it.
   A down
   B off
   C out
   D up

40 I'll give you a call ___ the next hour or so.
   A within
   B without
   C among
   D along

Unit 13

Awareness

1 Which of these sentences are correct (C) and incorrect (I)?

1 Our car was stole last week. ___
2 I'm being attacked by a gang of youths. ___
3 The suspect is been taken to the police station. ___
4 You'll be being given a new identity badge. ___
5 What will be done about the problems in our area? ___
6 This project must be finished by next week. ___
7 He is believed that crime is falling. ___
8 This street hasn't been cleaned for weeks. ___
9 This area is being said to be the safest in the city. ___
10 You won't be told about our decision until this evening. ___

How many did you get right? ☐

Grammar

Passive Voice: Tenses

We use the passive when
- the action is more important than who or what is responsible for it (the agent).
*The terrorist **was arrested** yesterday evening.*
- we don't know the agent, or it is not important.
*Surveys **are used** to investigate people's preferences.*

The passive is formed with the verb *be* and a past participle. Notice how the active verb forms change to passive verb forms.

Tense	Active	Passive
Present Simple	take/takes	am/are/is taken
Present Continuous	am/are/is taking	am/are/is being taken
Past Simple	took	was/were taken
Past Continuous	was/were taking	was/were being taken
Present Perfect Simple	have/has taken	have/has been taken
Past Perfect Simple	had taken	had been taken
Future Simple	will take	will be taken

We change an active sentence into a passive sentence in the following way.

The object of the verb in the active sentence becomes the subject of the verb in the passive sentence. The verb *be* is used in the same tense of the main verb in the active sentence, together with the past participle of the main verb in the active sentence.
*They **were testing** him. He **was being tested**.*

In this example we do not know who was testing him and it is not very important, so we do not include this information in the passive sentence.

> **Note**
>
> When it is important to mention the agent in a passive sentence, we use the word *by*. When we want to mention a tool or material in the passive sentence, we use the word *with*.
>
> *The children **broke** a vase.*
> *A vase **was broken by** the children.*
> *The dog **was hit by** a car.*
> *All ambulances **are fitted with** sirens.*

> **Note**
>
> There is no passive form for Future Continuous, Present Perfect Continuous and Past Perfect Continuous.

> **Note**
>
> When we want to change an active sentence with two objects into the passive voice, one becomes the subject of the passive sentence and the other one remains an object. Which object we choose depends on what we want to emphasise. If the personal object remains an object in the passive sentence, then we have to use a suitable preposition (*to, for,* etc).
>
> *We gave **her** the **documents**.*
> *She **was given** the documents.*
> *The documents **were given to** her.*

Passive Voice: Gerunds, Infinitives & Modal Verbs

Tense	Active	Passive
Gerund	taking	being taken
Bare infinitive	take	be taken
Full infinitive	to take	to be taken
Modal	can take	can be taken

My brother hates **being told** off.
This job **had better be completed** by the end of today.
She agreed **to be transferred** to another police station.
All new students **must be given** a guided tour on their first day.

Note
We often use verbs like *believe, consider, know, expect, say, suppose* and *think* in the passive voice. They can be used in an impersonal or a personal passive structure.

We form the impersonal passive structure with *it* + passive verb + *that* + clause.
Many people believe that poverty increases crime.
It is believed that poverty increases crime.

We form the personal structure with noun + passive verb + full infinitive.
Many people say that pets help you to relax.
Pets are said to help you to relax.

Grammar Exercises

2 Circle the correct words.

1. My car is **been / being** serviced at the moment.
2. Two young men were **killing / killed** yesterday in a car accident.
3. My father is going to be **promoted / promote** next week.
4. He has never **be / been** suspected of theft before.
5. Our teacher will **be taught / have been teaching** for 25 years when she retires.
6. Two football fans were **arrested / arresting** yesterday.
7. A window was **broke / broken** at school yesterday and I was **accusing / accused** of doing it.
8. Our mail is **delivering / delivered** to our doorstep every day.
9. Smoking **doesn't / isn't** allowed in hospitals.
10. The boy was **took / taken** to the hospital immediately after the accident.

3 Put the sentences into the passive.

1. They build a house.
   A house _____.
2. They are building a house.
   A house _____.
3. They built a house.
   A house _____.
4. They were building a house.
   A house _____.
5. They have built a house.
   A house _____.
6. They had built a house.
   A house _____.
7. They will build a house.
   A house _____.
8. They are going to build a house.
   A house _____.
9. They will have built a house.
   A house _____.

Unit 13

4 Complete the sentences with the correct form, active or passive, of the verbs in brackets.

1. A postcard _____ (send) to me yesterday.
2. Sam _____ (not invite) me to his party last Saturday.
3. A gift _____ (deliver) to him by post.
4. He _____ (paint) his bedroom at the moment. He can't speak to you.
5. This dress can't _____ (wash) by hand. It should _____ (take) to the dry cleaner's.
6. They _____ (bring) up their children in France, but now they live in Italy.
7. Your watch can't _____ (repair). You should _____ (buy) a new one.
8. Your letter _____ (not post) yet.

5 Rewrite the sentences in the passive.

1. Pupils mustn't chew gum in the classroom.
   Gum _____.
2. He must deliver this parcel right away.
   This _____.
3. He can't have broken the vase.
   The _____.
4. We must wear formal clothes to the reception.
   Formal clothes _____.
5. She has to make all the preparations for the party.
   All the preparations _____.
6. We don't have to clean the bedroom now.
   The bedroom _____.
7. We should take the child to his parents' house.
   The child _____.
8. People can bring their pets to the hotel.
   Pets _____.
9. They ought to build a new school in our town.
   A new school _____.
10. He might have taken the book by mistake.
    The book _____.

6 Rewrite the sentences.

1. They believe that smoking causes cancer.
   a It _is believed that smoking causes cancer_.
   b Smoking _is believed to cause cancer_.
2. They say that Emma plays the violin very well.
   a It _____.
   b Emma _____.
3. They expect that Jude Law will win the Oscar for Best Actor.
   a It _____.
   b Jude Law _____.
4. People know that he trains very hard.
   a It _____.
   b He _____.
5. People understand that politicians sometimes lie.
   a It _____.
   b Politicians _____.
6. They think that a hurricane is heading in this direction.
   a It _____.
   b A hurricane _____.

7 Complete the second sentence so that it has a similar meaning to the first sentence. Use the word in bold.

1 They told you to be here at ten.
  be
  You _____ at ten.

2 They are investigating the case at the moment.
  is
  The case _____ at the moment.

3 They have just redecorated their room.
  been
  Their room _____ redecorated.

4 They might pull down that old cinema.
  pulled
  That old cinema _____ down.

5 They brought their children up in Italy.
  were
  Their children _____ in Italy.

6 You had better tidy your room before you go to bed.
  tidied
  This room _____ before you go to bed.

7 They grow rice in China.
  grown
  Rice _____ in China.

8 I hate it when my brother tickles me.
  stand
  I can't _____ by my brother.

Vocabulary

Phrasal verbs

8 Match the phrasal verbs with their meanings.

1 hold up
2 hold on
3 do away with
4 do up
5 do without
6 give yourself up
7 give away
8 pass away

a to wait for a short while
b to kill or get rid of
c to surrender to the police
d to rob
e to fix or decorate something, so that it looks good
f to manage without something
g to die
h to give something to someone for free

9 Complete the sentences with the correct form of the phrasal verbs from 8.

1 I don't think I could _____ my laptop. I need it for my work.
2 They are _____ free bottles of water in the park today.
3 Three men _____ the bank in the high street this afternoon, but they were soon arrested.
4 Can you _____ for a minute? I just need to deal with this client.
5 The kidnappers finally _____, and are now in jail.
6 My grandfather _____ peacefully in his sleep at the age of 85.
7 Have you heard that they are _____ the old clubhouse, and hope to open it to the public again in the summer?
8 The pupils at our school hope to _____ the school uniform soon, because it is very unpopular.

Unit 13 93

Unit 13

Prepositions

10 Circle the correct words.

1 You can't do that – it's **against / under / to** the law.
2 Barry is **against / under / to** suspicion of having taken part in a robbery.
3 The people are starting to campaign **against / under / to** high taxes.
4 Come with us, Sir. You are **against / under / to** arrest.
5 The murderer was sentenced **against / under / to** a lifetime in prison.
6 **Against / Under / To** my mind, the best way to reduce crime is to reduce poverty.

Collocations & Expressions

11 Complete the sentences with these words.

| advantage bars guilty knowledge law responsibility |

1 You have to take _____ for your actions – you can't blame anyone else.
2 It is common _____ that Richard Brown is the leader of a criminal gang.
3 It is awful that some criminals will take _____ of old people and rob them of their life savings.
4 Finally, they caught the con man and put him behind _____ for eight years.
5 If you are found _____, you will have to pay a large fine.
6 He is one of the few people I know who got rich without breaking the _____!

Words easily confused

12 Use the words given to complete the sentences underneath. Make sure the words are in the correct form. Use each word at least once.

1 | glance sight view vision |

   a Just one _____ at the patient was enough to prompt the doctor to call an ambulance.
   b Make sure we get a room with a sea _____.
   c Stay out of _____ until they've gone.
   d These glasses will improve your _____.
   e We left the port, hoping to catch _____ of at least one whale.

2 | crossing cruise expedition passage |

   a Going on a world _____ sounds like fun.
   b Scott led a(n) _____ to the North Pole.
   c The _____ from the mainland to the island takes two hours.
   d Only the Red Cross workers were guaranteed safe _____ through the war-torn country.

3 | inhabitant neighbour resident tenant |

   a They don't own the flat. They're _____.
   b I'm afraid parking is for _____ only.
   c Our next-door _____ have a party at least once a week.
   d The _____ of this island have some very strange customs.

4 | earth ground land soil |

   a Sandy _____ is no good for growing these flowers.
   b I found the bracelet lying on the _____ outside.
   c Her family owns quite a lot of _____.
   d What on _____ are you doing?

Word formation mixed

13 Use the word in capitals to form a word that fits in the gap.

1 Have you heard about the _____ at the local shop today? **ROB**
2 I have always suspected that Mark was a _____. **CRIME**
3 With a dangerous driver at the wheel, a car becomes a _____ weapon. **DEAD**
4 _____ is a problem for governments and citizens the world over. **TERROR**
5 We provide towels and washing facilities for the _____ of our guests. **CONVENIENT**
6 Offering money to a police officer is a serious _____. **OFFEND**
7 It is almost impossible to destroy this watch – it's _____. **BREAK**
8 We recently learnt that my great grandfather was a _____ thief. **PROFESSION**

Sentence transformation

14 Complete the second sentence so that it has a similar meaning to the first sentence, using the word given. Do not change the word given. You must use between two and five words.

1 They believe the event will be a huge success.
   believed
   It _____ will be a huge success.

2 Your dog can't have eaten your homework!
   been
   Your homework _____ by your dog!

3 They say Tonya is a great dancer.
   said
   Tonya _____ a great dancer.

4 She hates it when people lie to her.
   stand
   She _____ to.

5 You don't have to pay the bill straight away.
   paid
   The bill _____ paid straight away.

6 It is time to get rid of this stupid law.
   away
   It is time _____ this stupid law.

7 My bicycle is essential to me.
   without
   I couldn't _____ my bicycle.

8 People suspect he's a terrorist.
   suspicion
   He's _____ a terrorist.

9 They put him in jail for his crime.
   bars
   They put him _____ for his crime.

Unit 14

Awareness

1 Which of these sentences are correct (C) and incorrect (I)?

1. We have had smoke alarms installed in every room. ___
2. I'm used to have my hair cut every month. ___
3. He got his wallet stolen when he was on holiday. ___
4. We'll have our car serviced soon. ___
5. Did you get your photo taken by the police? ___
6. Have you have had your eyebrows trimmed? ___
7. They were getting their bikes repaired when I saw them. ___
8. What time are you to having your fingernails polished? ___
9. She lost her passport, but got it replaced within a week. ___
10. Did you use to get your mum to clean your shoes? ___

How many did you get right? ☐

Grammar
Causative

We use the causative
- to say that someone has arranged for somebody to do something for them.
*Many people **have** locks **fitted** to their garage doors.*
- to say that something unpleasant happened to someone.
*We **had** our flat **broken into** while we were on holiday.*

We form the causative with *have* + object + past participle.
It can be used in a variety of tenses. When we want to mention the agent, we use the word *by*.
*We **have had** new windows **fitted**.*
*My grandmother **used to have** her piano **tuned** once a year.*
*You **will have** your passport **checked** (by passport control).*

> **Note**
> We can also use *get* + object + past participle.
> This structure is less formal. However, when we talk about unpleasant events, we must use *have*.
> *I **got** my glasses **repaired** at the optician's.*

Grammar Exercises

2 Circle the correct words.

1. Dad **had / has got** his car washed yesterday.
2. It's going to be a hot summer. We must **get / to have** air conditioning put in.
3. It's three years since we last had the bedroom walls **paint / painted**.
4. I **get / 'm getting** my computer fixed at the moment.
5. Terry is going **to have / get** her dad check her work before she hands it in.
6. The inspector **is having / to get** the whole house checked for fingerprints.
7. Sally **had / got** her arm broken in a climbing accident.
8. I'll **have / get** a plumber to have a look at our bathroom taps.

3 Complete the sentences using the causative form.

1 We _____ last week. (our roof / repair)
2 She _____ yet. (not / her passport photo / take)
3 He _____ at the moment. (his eyes / test)
4 They _____ when I called in this morning. (the alarm / check)
5 Ray _____ once a year. (his carpets / clean)
6 We _____ once since we moved in. (the flat / redecorate)
7 I _____ by nine o'clock yesterday. (already my eyes / test)
8 I have called a plumber. He _____ before you arrive. (the tap / fix)

4 Rewrite the sentences using the causative form.

1 Someone stole my camera.
   I _____.
2 They are servicing my car.
   I _____.
3 Someone broke into my aunt's house.
   My aunt _____.
4 The hairdresser is going to cut my hair tomorrow.
   I am _____.
5 An electrician fixed the TV for Mary.
   Mary _____.
6 The dentist is filling one of my teeth.
   I am _____.

5 Write questions for the answers in bold.

1 _____?
   I have my hair cut by **my brother**.
2 _____?
   I'm going to get **Mr Walker** to service my car.
3 _____?
   I had my room painted **last month**.
4 _____?
   I need to get **my watch** fixed.
5 _____?
   I get my little sister to clean **my room**.
6 _____?
   I have my teeth checked **every six months**.
7 _____?
   I've had my computer upgraded **because it was so slow**.
8 _____?
   I'll be having my dress made **at *Divine Designs***.

Unit 14 97

Unit 14

6 Complete the second sentence so that it has a similar meaning to the first sentence. Use the word in bold.

1 They have already published three books of mine.
  had
  I've _____ three books published by them.

2 We had our boiler fixed by a plumber.
  got
  We _____ our boiler.

3 Our floor needs polishing before the party.
  polished
  We must _____ before the party.

4 Tom's mother washes his clothes.
  gets
  Tom _____ his mother.

5 Is someone going to fix your teeth for you?
  have
  Are you _____ fixed?

6 They will deliver Carol's new fridge tomorrow.
  delivered
  Carol will _____ tomorrow.

Vocabulary

Phrasal verbs

7 Match the phrasal verbs with their meanings.

1 own up   a to put somebody in prison
2 put away   b to realise someone is trying to trick you
3 put down   c to deceive somebody
4 put off   d to admit to doing something wrong
5 see through   e to write someone's name on a document
6 see to   f to make someone dislike something
7 take in   g to have similar characteristics to an older family member
8 take after   h to deal with something that needs attention

8 Complete the sentences with the correct form of the phrasal verbs from 7.

1 He tried to trick me, but I _____ his plan.
2 Sam _____ his father – he is a thief and a liar!
3 I think Tommy broke your computer, but he'll never _____ to it.
4 They caught the murderer and _____ him _____ for 25 years.
5 Shall I _____ your name for the neighbourhood watch scheme?
6 Don't worry about the leaking tap – I'll _____ it when I get home.
7 Were you really _____ by that salesman's speech?
8 I was going to go south for the weekend, but I was _____ by the bad weather reports.

Prepositions

9 Circle the correct words.

1 Nobody likes being accused **of / from / in** a crime they didn't commit.
2 I picked up the gun and hid it **of / from / in** sight under a cushion.
3 She kicked the man in the leg **of / from / in** self-defense.
4 I'll give you this CD **of / from / in** exchange for that book.
5 After he was caught speeding through town, my uncle was banned **of / from / in** driving for six months.
6 It was very thoughtful **of / from / in** you to offer to help Mary after her accident.

Collocations & Expressions

10 Complete the sentences with these words.

| burglar   community   court   crime   jury   life |

1 Steve had to do _____ service when he got caught painting graffiti on the park walls.
2 If they ever catch the killer, he'll be given a _____ sentence.
3 I have to take at least a week off work to do _____ duty next month.
4 You really ought to get a _____ alarm fitted on your house.
5 His _____ case is coming up soon. I hope they find him innocent!
6 This town is suffering a _____ wave at the moment.

Words easily confused

11 Use the words given to complete the sentences underneath. Make sure the words are in the correct form. Use each word at least once.

1 | contain   form   hold   include   involve |
  a My job _____ travelling abroad quite frequently.
  b The price _____ airport taxes and transfers.
  c Wood _____ only a small part of the structure of these houses.
  d Nobody knew exactly what the box _____.
  e We need a tank that can _____ at least ten gallons.

2 | inland   inner   interior   internal |
  a We'd better get an _____ decorator to do the work.
  b His injuries are superficial and there's no _____ bleeding.
  c The village is about ten miles _____, not on the coast.
  d There is a great deal of poverty in _____ city areas.

3 | carry out   celebrate   hold   perform |
  a A soldier must _____ orders without question.
  b They're _____ their silver wedding anniversary.
  c The next meeting will be _____ on 2 March.
  d He enjoys _____ magic tricks at children's birthday parties.

4 | sale   discount   bargain   offer |
  a There's a(n) _____ of 20% on all cameras this week.
  b It was on special _____; that's why I only paid £10 for it.
  c Wait until the _____ start before you go shopping for clothes.
  d I got a real _____ on these shoes – they were half price!

Unit 14

Word formation verb → noun

12 Use the word in capitals to form a word that fits in the gap.

1. The police had to let him go because they had no _____ that he had committed a crime. **PROVE**
2. Have you come to any _____ about the court case yet? **CONCLUDE**
3. Being a police officer can be quite a dangerous _____. **OCCUPY**
4. When Philip graduated, he became a professional _____. **PHOTOGRAPH**
5. She had to have an _____ to correct her broken ankle. **OPERATE**
6. We didn't realise the _____ of the news at the time. **SIGNIFY**
7. This hotel has become very busy since it got a _____ in a national newspaper. **RECOMMEND**
8. The high crime rate in the area influenced our _____ to move to the country. **DECIDE**

Sentence transformation

13 Complete the second sentence so that it has a similar meaning to the first sentence, using the word given. Do not change the word given. You must use between two and five words.

1. She always has her hair cut by her aunt.
   gets
   She always _____ her hair.
2. Our grass needs cutting this weekend.
   cut
   We should _____ this weekend.
3. Somebody will remove your plaster tomorrow.
   removed
   You _____ tomorrow.
4. I saw Gary sing and now I don't like him anymore.
   put
   Seeing Gary sing _____ him.
5. You'll get put in prison for a long time.
   away
   They'll _____ for a long time.
6. Mary's father is very like her in many ways.
   after
   Mary _____ in many ways.
7. I'll swap my skateboard for your BMX.
   exchange
   I'll give you my skateboard _____ your BMX.
8. Someone will deal with this problem tomorrow.
   seen
   I'll get this problem _____ tomorrow.

Unit 15

Awareness

1 Which of these sentences are correct (C) and incorrect (I)?

1. If you'll fall off your bike, you'll hurt yourself. ___
2. If you climb to the top, you'll be able to see the sea. ___
3. I won't put her in the team unless she'll train harder. ___
4. I'd buy the coat if I thought it suited me. ___
5. She wouldn't shout so much if she would behave herself. ___
6. If he hadn't missed his flight, he wouldn't have had to buy another ticket. ___
7. If you would have had a map, you wouldn't have got lost. ___
8. If I was you, I'd apologise immediately. ___
9. If you boil water, it would turn into steam. ___
10. Don't tell Wendy about the party if she phones. ___

How many did you get right? ☐

Grammar

Zero Conditional

If clause	Main clause
present simple	present simple

We use the zero conditional to talk about an action or situation that is always true. We can use *when* instead of *if*.
If you **drive** a car, you **pollute** the atmosphere.
When you **drive** a car, you **pollute** the atmosphere.

First Conditional

If clause	Main clause
present tense	will + bare infinitive

We use the first conditional to talk about an action or situation that will probably happen now or in the future.
If the volcano **erupts**, the village **will be destroyed**.
If the climate **gets** warmer, the sea level **will rise**.

We can use *can*, *could*, *may* or *might* in the main clause instead of *will*. We can also use an imperative.
If you want to help your dad, you **could mow** the lawn.
If you don't want to get into trouble, **behave** yourself.

Unit 15 **101**

Unit 15

Second Conditional

If clause	Main clause
past tense	would + bare infinitive

We use the second conditional to talk about an action or a situation
• that is unlikely to happen now or in the future.
If I **had** the time, I **would write** a book.
• that is impossible or imaginary in the present or in the future.
If I **had** a million pounds, I **would buy** that house.

We can also use the second conditional to give advice.
If I **were** you, I**'d buy** an electric car.

We can use *could* or *might* in the main clause instead of *would*.
You **could swim** with dolphins if you went to Florida.
I **might be able** to afford it if you gave me more pocket money.

> **Note**
> We usually use *were* for all persons in second conditional sentences.
> *If my son **were** older, he'd be allowed to see this film.*

Third Conditional

If clause	Main clause
past perfect tense	would + have + past participle

We use the third conditional to talk about events or situations in the past that could have happened, but didn't. These are always hypothetical things because we cannot change the past.
If my dad **had gone** to university, he **would have been** a teacher. (He didn't go to university, so he isn't a teacher.)

We can use *could* or *might* in the main clause instead of *would*.
We **could have won** the championship if we hadn't lost the final game.
If the meeting had been earlier, I **might have been** there.

Grammar Exercises

2 Circle the correct words.

1. If you are caught speeding, you **would get / get** a fine.
2. She **would / will** pass the exam if she studies hard.
3. Sheila **didn't damage / wouldn't have damaged** the car if she had been more careful.
4. Unless she **stops / doesn't stop** eating now, she will feel sick.
5. If you **took / are taking** more exercise, you would feel better.
6. If the baby **is / were** a girl, I'll call her Emily.
7. Sally **would be / is** very happy if she were offered the job.

3 Complete the sentences using the First Conditional.

1. If I _____ (find) your notebook, I _____ (give) it to you.
2. If you _____ (not know) the meaning of a word, you _____ (look) in a dictionary.
3. We _____ (go) for a picnic if the weather _____ (be) nice tomorrow.
4. They _____ (believe) you even if you _____ (tell) them the truth.
5. I _____ (wash) the dishes if you _____ (be) tired.
6. We _____ (not get) any tickets for the rock concert unless we _____ (go) much earlier.
7. If the dog _____ (not stop) barking, our neighbours _____ (call) the police again.
8. She _____ (not come) to the party if you _____ (not invite) her.

4 Complete the second sentences using the Second Conditional.

1. Sally doesn't work very hard; that's why she doesn't earn much money.
   If she _____ harder, she _____ more money.
2. He smokes a lot; that's why he's coughing so much.
   If he _____ a lot, he _____ so much.
3. She doesn't speak any foreign languages; that's why she can't find a job.
   She _____ if she _____ a foreign language.
4. I get up late every morning, so I am always late for school.
   I _____ late for school if I _____ every morning.
5. He doesn't have much free time, so he doesn't see his friends very often.
   If he _____ more free time, he _____ his friends more often.
6. They play loud music every night; that's why we can't sleep.
   If they _____ loud music every night, we _____.
7. The food is too salty and I can't eat it.
   I _____ the food if it _____ so salty.
8. You can't take any photos because the camera is broken.
   If the camera _____, you _____ some photos.

5 Complete the sentences using the Third Conditional.

1. If you _____ (pay) the fine, you _____ (not be) sent to prison.
2. If I _____ (know) that dogs were allowed in this luxurious hotel, I _____ (bring) mine.
3. Sorry! I _____ (not drop by) if you _____ (tell) me you were busy.
4. If I _____ (see) you at the bus stop, I _____ (pick) you up in my car.
5. We _____ (go) by air if we _____ (have) enough money.
6. I _____ (call) you if I _____ (not lose) your telephone number.
7. We _____ (not take) a taxi if the buses _____ (not be) on strike.
8. I _____ (take) the children to the beach if it _____ (not rain).
9. If I _____ (know) it would spoil my appetite, I _____ (not eat) it.
10. He _____ (not make) so many mistakes if he _____ (be) more careful.

6 Complete the second sentence so that it has a similar meaning to the first sentence.

1. Don't eat so much and you will lose weight.
   If you _____.
2. Can I borrow your bike? I can give it back to you this afternoon.
   If you _____.
3. Julie can't drink coffee because she gets a headache.
   When _____.
4. Why don't you talk to her about your problem?
   If I were you, _____.
5. We didn't have enough money to go out because we spent too much on holiday.
   If we _____.
6. I was listening to my stereo, so I didn't hear the telephone ring.
   If I _____.

Unit 15

Unit 15

7 Complete the sentences with the word that best fits each gap.
1. I wouldn't be so confident if I _____ him.
2. She would _____ got a promotion if she had worked harder.
3. My mum doesn't travel by plane because she _____ afraid of flying.
4. _____ I had your email address, I'd have sent you the photo.
5. If I have enough time, I _____ come and visit you – but I can't be sure.
6. When you put salt on ice, _____ melts.
7. I won't call him if he _____ still working.
8. If you come with us, we _____ have to book a bigger table at the restaurant.

Vocabulary

Phrasal verbs

8 Match the phrasal verbs with their meanings.
1. beaver away
2. block out
3. blow over
4. blow up
5. burst into
6. clam up
7. horse around
8. talk into

a to refuse to say anything
b to stop light or noise passing through
c to persuade someone to do something
d to work hard at something
e to destroy with a bomb
f to suddenly start
g to play in a silly or noisy way
h (of a storm or argument) to end without causing harm

9 Complete the sentences with the correct form of the phrasal verbs from 8.
1. We were lucky that the storm _____ quickly.
2. It wasn't easy, but I finally _____ my parents _____ buying me a scooter.
3. The tree _____ flames when it was struck by lightning.
4. The suspect was quite talkative at first, but he _____ when the sergeant entered the room.
5. I need some thick curtains to _____ the sunshine in the morning.
6. Terrorists _____ the central post office last night.
7. Ted spent the afternoon _____ on his car in the garage.
8. If those children don't stop _____, I'll send them to bed early!

Prepositions

10 Circle the correct words.
1. Unfortunately, this tiny umbrella doesn't offer much protection **from / with / of** the rain.
2. It's very difficult to live with the threat **from / with / of** war every day.
3. I'm not sure that I can cope **from / with / of** another exam so soon after the last one!
4. Is the customer satisfied **from / with / of** his new machine?
5. The headmaster will be made aware **from / with / of** your behaviour.
6. Don't let Simon discourage you **from / with / of** joining the club.

Collocations & Expressions

11 Complete the sentences with these words.

> example   heart   impression   nerves   respect   sight

1 I was under the _____ that Gary wanted to take part in this project.
2 You should recycle as much as you can to set a(n) _____ for the rest of the neighbourhood.
3 At first _____, Amelia's new hairstyle looked like a hat!
4 The noise our washing machine makes when it stops really gets on my _____.
5 She believes, with all her _____, that one day she will be an Olympic champion.
6 The local school has, in one _____, improved a great deal in recent years.

Words easily confused

12 Use the words given to complete the sentences underneath. Make sure the words are in the correct form. Use each word at least once.

1 course   dessert   meal   starter
   a Breakfast is the most important _____ of the day.
   b Apple pie and ice cream is my favourite _____.
   c For the main _____ I would like a steak.
   d I'll have soup for a _____, please.

2 aisle   corridor   line   row
   a Why are you in the _____ when you should be in your classroom?
   b They live in a street with two neat _____ of identical bungalows.
   c I prefer a window seat to a(n) _____ seat when I'm flying.
   d Don't walk on the railway _____.
   e The bride looked nervous as she walked down the _____.

3 consider   guess   reckon   wonder
   a I _____ what Bob's done with the TV guide.
   b Would you _____ a career in the army?
   c Can you _____ how many people came to the party?
   d He _____ he's a much better footballer than me.

4 display   show   demonstration   exhibition
   a Reg Hawkins has won first prize in the flower _____ yet again.
   b It was the best firework _____ I have ever seen.
   c Give us a(n) _____ of how the machine works.
   d All the major manufacturers were represented at the computer _____.

Word formation   verb → adjective

13 Use the word in capitals to form a word that fits in the gap.

1 This phone is completely _____ without a battery.   **USE**
2 We watched a very _____ documentary about whales last night.   **EDUCATE**
3 Hang-gliding is a very _____ sport – I wouldn't like to try it.   **RISK**
4 Neil is the most _____ person I know – he'll do anything for you.   **HELP**
5 Your behaviour is totally _____, and if it doesn't change, you will have to leave.   **ACCEPT**
6 What an _____ show that was!   **OUTRAGE**
7 The police thanked the witness for being so _____.   **COOPERATE**
8 She didn't get the job because, although she had the qualifications, she was _____.   **EXPERIENCE**

Unit 15

Sentence transformation

14 Complete the second sentence so that it has a similar meaning to the first sentence, using the word given. Do not change the word given. You must use between two and five words.

1. The wall fell down because you didn't build it properly.
   had
   If _____ properly, it wouldn't have fallen down.

2. We won't finish this job without Bob's help.
   us
   If _____ , we won't finish this job.

3. It only works if you turn it on.
   unless
   It _____ you turn it on.

4. My advice to you is to forget about it.
   were
   If _____ forget about it.

5. Molly was finally persuaded to come with us.
   talked
   We finally _____ with us.

6. I'm going to let the boss know about this.
   aware
   I'm going to _____ of this.

7. It irritates me that she takes offence so easily.
   nerves
   It _____ that she takes offence so easily.

8. He is completely convinced that he is a great writer.
   heart
   He believes _____ that he is a great writer.

Unit 16

Awareness

1 Which of these sentences are correct (C) and incorrect (I)?

1. Provided everyone agrees, we'll leave early today. ___
2. If you hadn't told me, I still don't know. ___
3. She won't be able to help you otherwise she's busy. ___
4. As long it doesn't cost too much, I'll buy it. ___
5. Supposing we have some spare time, where shall we go? ___
6. If he hadn't taken the wrong road, he'd be here by now. ___
7. You are earning more money today if you had gone to university. ___
8. He'll do the work on condition that you pay him in advance. ___
9. I'm happy to come with you, provided my parents would give me permission. ___
10. Be quiet, otherwise you won't know what to do. ___

How many did you get right? ☐

Grammar

Mixed Conditionals

If clause	Main clause
past perfect tense	would + bare infinitive

A mixed conditional is where the two clauses in a conditional sentence refer to different times. We use a mixed conditional to express the present result of a hypothetical past event or situation.
If our car **hadn't been stolen**, we**'d be** home in bed by now.

Conditionals without *if*

We can use *provided/providing that*, *on condition that* and *as long as* to replace *if* in first conditional sentences.
Provided I have the time, I'll come and visit you this evening.
On condition that you promise to behave, we'll go to the beach tomorrow.
As long as the head teacher doesn't object, we'll use the hall for rehearsals.

We can use *unless* in first and second conditional sentences. It means the same as *if not*.
She won't get to the meeting on time **unless** she gets a taxi.
Unless you have studied for years, you will never speak a foreign language fluently.

We can use *otherwise* to replace an *if* clause. It means *if not*.
If you don't drive more carefully, I'm not getting in the car with you.
Drive more carefully. **Otherwise**, I'm not getting in the car with you.

We can use *supposing* in all conditional sentences. The main clause is usually a question. It means *imagine* or *what if*.
Supposing you could live anywhere in the world, where would you choose?
Supposing we had run out of money, what would we have done?
Supposing you were a millionaire, what would you do with your money?

Unit 16

Grammar Exercises

2 Complete the sentences with the correct form of the verb in brackets.
1. If we _____ (not miss) our flight, we would be lying in the sunshine right now.
2. You _____ (not be) so tired now if you had gone to bed earlier.
3. My dad would be rich now if he _____ (buy) the company years ago.
4. This town would still be beautiful if it _____ (not be) bombed in the war.
5. If he had joined an athletics club when he was a boy, he _____ (be) a champion runner by now.
6. If you _____ (be) born in China, you'd speak fluent Mandarin.

3 Circle the correct words.
1. **Provided / Unless / Otherwise** we have enough money, we'll go to France on holiday.
2. You'll never succeed **on condition that / unless / otherwise** you work a lot harder.
3. We'd better hurry up, **provided / unless / otherwise** we'll be late.
4. **As long as / Unless / Supposing** it rains tomorrow, the whole family is going on a picnic.
5. Steven agreed to wash my bicycle, **on condition that / unless / otherwise** I helped him with his maths.
6. **Provided / Unless / Supposing** you lost your job tomorrow, what would you do?
7. You'll be fine **as long as / supposing / otherwise** you do exactly as I say.
8. Let's not stay too long, **on condition that / otherwise / unless** we won't get home before dark.

4 Complete the second sentence so that it has a similar meaning to the first sentence.
1. If you don't stop crying, I won't help you.
   Unless _____.
2. If you don't stop complaining, I won't let you go out again.
   Unless _____.
3. We won't be able to sit together if we don't get on the boat now.
   Unless _____.
4. We won't go swimming if it's not hot.
   Unless _____.
5. If you don't ask him, he won't help you.
   Unless _____.
6. If she doesn't go to hospital immediately, her life will be in danger.
   Unless _____.

5 Complete the sentences with the correct form of the verbs in brackets.
1. Supposing she _____ (see) you two together, how would she react?
2. Supposing they hadn't won the championship, _____ the manager _____ (lose) his job?
3. Supposing there aren't any applicants for the job, how _____ you _____ (fill) the vacancy?
4. Supposing she _____ (apologise), will you two be friends again?
5. Supposing he hadn't been willing to lie for you, how _____ you _____ (explain) the situation?
6. Supposing there _____ (be) a storm, where would they have found shelter?

6 Complete the sentences with the word that best fits each gap.

1. Don't say anything to Sammy about this _____ he asks you – then you will have to.
2. Yes, you may borrow my car _____ long as you drive carefully.
3. _____ Tina trains hard, she stands a good chance of qualifying for the final.
4. He agreed to take the job on _____ that they gave him a new computer.
5. They'd be safely home by now if they _____ got on that last bus.
6. Supposing I gave you the money – what _____ you spend it on?
7. You'd better not be late, _____ Jane will be furious.

Vocabulary

Phrasal verbs

7 Match the phrasal verbs with their meanings.

1. freeze over ☐
2. figure out ☐
3. pig out ☐
4. take over ☐
5. rat on ☐
6. wear away ☐
7. wear out ☐
8. wipe out ☐

a. to eat too much food
b. (of surface of water) to turn to ice
c. to cause to become extinct
d. to find a solution after thinking about a problem
e. to be disloyal to somebody, especially by giving away a secret
f. to take control
g. to make somebody feel very tired
h. to make smaller or smoother over time

8 Complete the sentences with the correct form of the phrasal verbs from 7.

1. When our English teacher was ill, the French teacher _____ the class for a few days.
2. The kids aren't hungry because they _____ on biscuits and chocolate this afternoon.
3. Because everybody used to take a short cut over the field, they had _____ a path in the grass.
4. Many people are worried that tigers will be completely _____ by poachers.
5. We went skating on the lake which had _____ during the night.
6. The bank robber was furious when his friend _____ him to the police.
7. I finally _____ a way to solve this problem.
8. Hilda was _____ because she had been working hard all day.

Prepositions

9 Circle the correct words.

1. There has been a steep rise **in / on / to** the number of bicycle thefts in the area.
2. Fred is a very honest man – you can rely **in / on / to** him to tell you the truth.
3. It is important not to allow children to be exposed **in / on / to** too much violence in the cinema.
4. Does anyone object **in / on / to** the heating being turned up a bit?
5. Simone is really keen **in / on / to** saving the environment.
6. The head teacher's decision to do away with school uniform resulted **in / on / to** an increase in bad behaviour.

Unit 16

Collocations & Expressions

10 Complete the sentences with these words.

> bee   cat   crocodile   fish   wolf   worm

1 When you manage to get someone to tell you something against their will, you _____ the information out of them.
2 When someone is pretending to be sad, we say that they are crying _____ tears.
3 A dangerous person who is pretending to be harmless is a _____ in sheep's clothing.
4 When you are trying to encourage people to say something nice about you, you _____ for compliments.
5 Someone who is working very hard is as busy as a _____.
6 To let the _____ out of the bag means to accidentally reveal a big secret.

Words easily confused

11 Use the words given to complete the sentences underneath. Make sure the words are in the correct form. Use each word at least once.

1 > bar   lump   piece   sheet   slice

   a That's an interesting _____ of information.
   b Use a fresh _____ of paper for each question.
   c I'd like two _____ of ham in my sandwich.
   d How much sugar do you take, one _____ or two?
   e I've bought a _____ of chocolate for you.

2 > income   interest   investment   salary

   a The bank pays _____ on my account twice a year.
   b As the managing director of a large company she gets a large _____.
   c His _____ consists largely of rent he receives from property he owns.
   d Buying shares in mining wasn't considered a wise _____ at that time.

3 > branch   compartment   department   ward

   a During my stay in hospital I shared a _____ with nine other patients.
   b The train is nearly empty, with only a few passengers in each _____.
   c A new _____ of the bank is being opened here next week.
   d He works for a government _____, but I don't know which one.

4 > cure   heal   recover   treat

   a He was taken to Walton Hospital, where he was _____ for shock.
   b It'll take time for her to _____ from her injuries.
   c The wound _____ more quickly than I anticipated.
   d If this stuff doesn't _____ you, I don't know what will.

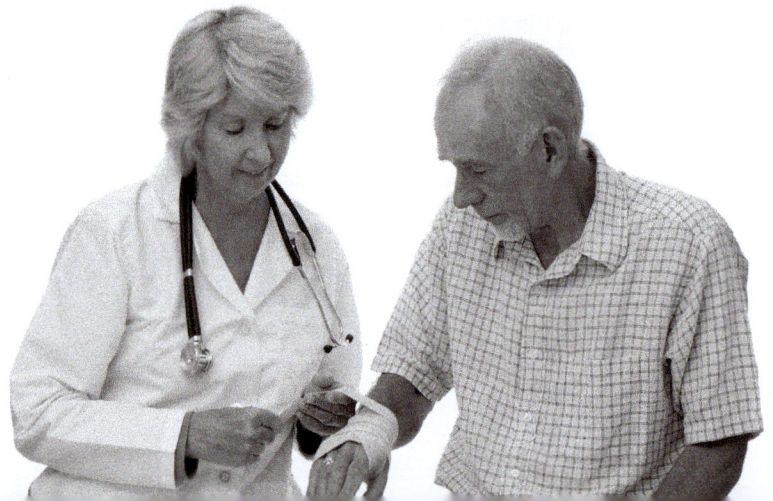

Word formation — adverbs

12 Use the word in capitals to form a word that fits in the gap.

1. We had a _____ awful holiday in Wales last winter. — **MEMORY**
2. The head teacher reacted _____ when he heard what Sam had done. — **FURY**
3. It's a pity they decorated the town centre so _____ – more people would visit if it looked nicer. — **ATTRACTIVE**
4. The dog quickly ate the food on the plate, and then looked _____ at its owner. — **GUILT**
5. The match ended _____, with the losing team claiming that they had been unfairly denied a penalty. — **CONTROVERSY**
6. Stop behaving so _____! — **FOOL**
7. The bus driver _____ steered the vehicle around the parked cars. — **SKILL**
8. The small boy _____ repeated the same question again and again, until his mother finally told him to shut up. — **IRRITATE**

Sentence transformation

13 Complete the second sentence so that it has a similar meaning to the first sentence, using the word given. Do not change the word given. You must use between two and five words.

1. If you don't finish your dinner, you aren't allowed to watch TV.
   unless
   You aren't allowed to watch TV _____ your dinner.
2. Supposing I hadn't been here to help you – what would you have done?
   if
   What _____ I hadn't been here to help you?
3. If you promise to be home before midnight, you can go to the party.
   long
   You can go to the party _____ to be home before midnight.
4. Provided I can return it if I don't like it, I'll buy your computer.
   condition
   I'll buy your computer _____ I can return it if I don't like it.
5. Did you solve the puzzle?
   figure
   Did you _____ to do the puzzle?
6. I'll drive if you are feeling too tired to continue.
   over
   I'll _____ the driving if you are feeling too tired to continue.
7. I can't believe he revealed the secret on live TV!
   cat
   I can't believe he _____ of the bag on live TV!
8. He's been looking after the children all day and now he's exhausted.
   worn
   He _____ after looking after the children all day.

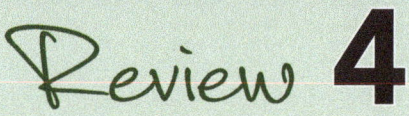

B2 Practice: FCE

Part 1

For questions 1–12, read the text below and decide which answer (A, B, C or D) best fits each gap. There is an example at the beginning (0).

Take care, it's a jungle out there

The **(0)** __ of young children playing happily in the garden is a joy to behold, especially when parents believe that they can come to no **(1)** __ there. If asked about possible dangers, parents will admit that children could be stung by a **(2)** __ of bees or scratch themselves on the rose bushes, but these are not **(3)** __ occurrences. In most people's **(4)** __, being at home means staying safe.

Unfortunately, the **(5)** __ points to quite a different story. About four thousand British toddlers are poisoned by plants each year. Some of them have to **(6)** __ time in hospital because their **(7)** __ is considered serious. Most parents are not **(8)** __ of which plants are poisonous. Often the flowers that are the most attractive are the most deadly, but it's no use trying to get this **(9)** __ to a small child!

Safety in the garden depends on parents paying close **(10)** __ to what their children are doing. When they are quiet, it often means they are **(11)** __ up to something. Although medical science in this day and **(12)** __ is likely to prevent a fatality, leaving children unattended in the garden is a big risk.

0	(A) sight	B scenery	C view	D vision
1	A injury	B harm	C damage	D hurt
2	A swarm	B pack	C flock	D shoal
3	A common	B many	C often	D usual
4	A idea	B attitude	C opinion	D thought
5	A fact	B proof	C testimony	D evidence
6	A spend	B earn	C pay	D win
7	A position	B condition	C situation	D location
8	A aware	B knowing	C conscious	D learnt
9	A back	B around	C into	D across
10	A notice	B attention	C attendance	D care
11	A going	B getting	C staying	D breaking
12	A time	B term	C age	D period

Part 2

For questions 13–24, read the text below and think of the word which best fits each gap. Use only one word in each gap. There is an example at the beginning (0).

A man with a vision

Stamford Raffles was born aboard a ship off the coast of Jamaica (0) __in__ 1781. Instead of attending university, he worked for the East India Company (13) _____ a clerk and studied hard in his spare (14) _____. At the age of 30, he became governor of Java, (15) _____ he employed zoologists and botanists (16) _____ discover all they could about the animals and plants on the islands. Raffles himself acquired a large collection of animals, including a Malayan sun bear that was brought (17) _____ with his children. The bear often joined Raffles for dinner, eating fruit (18) _____ drinking champagne.

On a trip to Europe in 1817, Raffles had the idea for the forming of a collection of living animals. (19) _____ founding the colony of Singapore in 1819, Raffles (20) _____ together with several influential scientists and aristocrats, (21) _____ listened carefully to his ideas. He convinced them, and he was voted president of (22) _____ Zoological Society of London. Raffles died suddenly from a stroke in 1826. Sadly, the man (23) _____ idea it was to start London Zoo did not see its opening two years (24) _____, in 1828.

Part 3

For questions 25–34, read the text below. Use the word given in capitals at the end of each line to form a word that fits in the gap in the same line. There is an example at the beginning (0).

A holiday on Mauritius

With holiday resorts the world over getting more (0) __crowded__, any	CROWD
place offering the opportunity of spending a holiday in a (25) _____	BEAUTY
luxury hotel next to (26) _____ sandy beaches is guaranteed to be	END
a major (27) _____. But where is one to find such a paradise in this	ATTRACT
day and age? Mauritius, an almost perfectly circular island about 600 miles from	
the East African coast, can provide a very (28) _____ location for	PLEASE
just such a holiday. The island, which is probably most famous as the home of the	
now-extinct dodo, has very little (29) _____ at this point in its history.	TOUR
This means that (30) _____ today can enjoy its unspoilt scenery	VISIT
in relative calm, undisturbed by fellow holiday makers who, let's face it, the discerning	
traveller does not want to associate with. It is true that there are not many sights on the	
island, but (31) _____ is never a problem since local organizations	BORE
offer exciting fishing and sailing trips to (32) _____ areas where you	HIDE
can see some of the most breathtaking natural (33) _____ in the	SCENE
world. Mauritius is guaranteed to leave the holiday maker (34) _____	COMPLETE
relaxed.	

Review 4

Part 4

For questions 35–42, complete the second sentence so that it has a similar meaning to the first sentence, using the word given. Do not change the word given. You must use between two and five words, including the word given. Here is an example (0).

Example:

0 You mustn't use a calculator in the test.
allowed
You are _____*not allowed to use*_____ a calculator in the test.

35 I'm still waiting for her decision.
decided
She _____ to do yet.

36 You are not allowed to take these documents out of the library.
remain
These documents _____ the library.

37 I've only got a little luggage, so I don't need a trolley.
much
I _____ luggage, so I don't need a trolley.

38 They are going to demolish the old shoe factory next month.
pulled
The old shoe factory is _____ next month.

39 I am sure he has told her my secret.
must
He _____ my secret.

40 Some of the paintings are still for sale.
been
Some of the paintings _____ yet.

41 He bought me a computer because I wanted to work at home.
so
He bought me a computer _____ work at home.

42 The goods cannot leave the factory unless there is a signature on these papers.
signed
These papers _____ the goods can leave the factory.

114

B2 Practice: ECCE

Grammar

For questions 1–20, choose the word or phrase that best completes the sentence or the conversation.

1. If I ___ you, I wouldn't eat that much.
   A were
   B am
   C be
   D was

2. You will ___ shown to your room by this gentleman.
   A be
   B being
   C have
   D having

3. We ___ new doors put in our house.
   A have had
   B have get
   C having
   D getting

4. If this car breaks down, we ___ be stuck here!
   A had
   B would have
   C will
   D can

5. ___ it rains tomorrow, what shall we do?
   A Providing
   B Supposing
   C Thinking
   D Imagining

6. You can wash the dishes, if you ___ to help.
   A are wanting
   B want
   C wanted
   D would want

7. As ___ as you are happy, I am happy too.
   A far
   B tall
   C long
   D wide

8. The bad news ___ given to my aunt.
   A is
   B was
   C were
   D are

9. He avoided ___ accused of fraud.
   A be
   B being
   C have
   D having

10. We hope ___ our new TV delivered today.
    A have
    B having
    C to have
    D had

11. He might be ___ to give you a lift.
    A can
    B able
    C how
    D want

12. You can't get in ___ you have a ticket.
    A unless
    B without
    C otherwise
    D would

13. We could ___ been the winners if we'd worked as a team.
    A of
    B had
    C would
    D have

14. We have to leave now, ___ we'll miss the bus.
    A unless
    B provided
    C otherwise
    D if

15. The boxer got his nose ___ in the fight.
    A broke
    B breaking
    C break
    D broken

16. I got my sister ___ my homework for me.
    A doing
    B to do
    C do
    D did

17. If you hadn't been sent off, we'd ___ holding that trophy now!
    A have
    B being
    C having
    D be

18. She'll do it, on ___ that you pay her.
    A situation
    B condition
    C provided
    D promise

19. They ___ all asked to participate.
    A be
    B were
    C have been
    D was

20. Look! I ___ my teeth whitened.
    A have
    B am having
    C have had
    D will get

Review 4 115

Review 4

Vocabulary

For questions 21–40, choose the word or phrase that most appropriately completes the sentence.

21 It's ___ the law to break the speed limit.
   A against
   B counter
   C versus
   D beside

22 He really ___ after his Uncle Tim.
   A takes
   B makes
   C holds
   D puts

23 She can see ___ your tricky scheme!
   A over
   B about
   C through
   D up

24 You can always rely ___ me to get the job finished on time.
   A of
   B to
   C for
   D on

25 The man turned out to be a wolf in ___ clothing.
   A dog's
   B cow's
   C goat's
   D sheep's

26 Are you ___ any suspicion for this crime?
   A with
   B under
   C over
   D beside

27 You should ___ yourself up to the police as soon as possible.
   A hold
   B put
   C give
   D take

28 I think it's time you ___ up to your crimes.
   A owned
   B showed
   C gave
   D turned

29 Mark will ___ over this project from now on, because I am giving up.
   A have
   B take
   C give
   D hold

30 Have you had a ___ alarm fitted?
   A robber
   B thief
   C criminal
   D burglar

31 Stop accusing me ___ cheating.
   A with
   B of
   C at
   D by

32 This, to my ___, is the best way to succeed.
   A brain
   B thought
   C idea
   D mind

33 They had an argument, but it had ___ over by the evening.
   A blown
   B burst
   C gone
   D flown

34 I was under the ___ that they were married.
   A impression
   B expression
   C confession
   D assessment

35 That smell is really ___ me off my food.
   A getting
   B throwing
   C moving
   D putting

36 Two robbers ___ up a jewellery store in town this afternoon.
   A took
   B went
   C brought
   D held

37 Let's go skating if the pond is frozen ___.
   A out
   B hard
   C over
   D up

38 The woolly mammoth was ___ out during the Ice Age.
   A swept
   B brushed
   C cleaned
   D wiped

39 She won't be able to cope ___ five children in the house!
   A on
   B after
   C with
   D at

40 I was talked ___ volunteering by my friends.
   A on
   B over
   C inside
   D into

Unit 17

Awareness

1 Which of these sentences are correct (**C**) and incorrect (**I**)?

1. She married a man her parents didn't approve of him. ____
2. I really like the car I bought last year. ____
3. Mr Fowler, that you met yesterday, is a famous author. ____
4. The singer you admire so much is only 16 years old. ____
5. The vacuum cleaner that you bought it is faulty. ____
6. The story that I told you is untrue. ____
7. That's the place when I grew up. ____
8. Do you remember the time where we first met? ____
9. Stella, who was my babysitter years ago, has just got married. ____
10. Nobody knows the reason why it happened. ____

How many did you get right? ☐

Grammar
Relative Clauses

Relative clauses give more information about the subject or the object of a sentence. They are introduced by the following words:
- *who* for people
- *which* for things
- *whose* to show possession
- *when* for time
- *where* for places
- *why* for reason

Defining Relative Clauses

This type of relative clause gives us information that we need to be able to understand who or what the speaker is talking about. We do not use commas to separate it from the rest of the sentence. We can use *that* instead of *who* and *which* in defining relative clauses.
*That's the school **where I learn English**.*
*We met some people **who/that were very nice**.*

When *who*, *which* or *that* is the object of the relative clause, we can omit the relative pronoun.
***She**'s the athlete (**who**) they selected for the national team.*
*The only **exam** (**which/that**) he didn't pass was French.*

Non-defining Relative Clauses

This type of relative clause gives us extra information which isn't necessary to understand the meaning of the main clause. We use commas to separate it from the rest of the sentence.
*Our new teacher, **who used to live in Portugal**, is very clever.*
*My geography project, **which is about the Far East**, has to be handed in tomorrow.*

Unit 17

Grammar Exercises

2 Circle the correct words.
1 Did you reply to the email **that / who** Mark sent you yesterday?
2 My mother was born at a time **when / which** her parents were very poor.
3 Mrs Jenkins, **who / that** is sitting at the back of the hall, is your new teacher.
4 That's the man **which / that** I spoke to yesterday.
5 Mrs Black, **which / whose** husband died two years ago, is in charge of the company.
6 He didn't tell us the reason **why / which** he left his job.
7 The restaurant **which / where** we usually eat is the best in town.
8 Early in the morning is the time **when / where** I like to go running.

3 Complete the sentences with the correct relative pronoun.
1 What is the name of the film star _____ won the Oscar for Best Actor this year?
2 The watch _____ I bought from your shop is not working anymore.
3 Does anyone know the reason _____ Tommy didn't turn up for training today?
4 Is that the place _____ they are going to build the new sports centre?
5 The film is about a woman _____ son suddenly disappears.
6 I'll never forget that summer _____ we all met for the first time.

4 Can we leave the pronouns out of these sentences? Write **Y** (yes) or **N** (no).
1 Tom, whose sister won the tennis championship, is very happy. ___
2 The gift that my friend gave me for my birthday was really great. ___
3 I met a woman whose father is a famous musician. ___
4 Please return the book which I lent you. ___
5 This is the house that they are going to knock down. ___
6 The supermarket where we usually shop is not too expensive. ___
7 The reason why I can't help you is because I am unwell. ___
8 My dad, who travels a lot on business, has visited many countries. ___

5 Join the sentences using a relative pronoun. Remember to add commas if the clause is non-defining.
1 Jenny is a successful lawyer. Her husband is unemployed.
   Jenny, whose husband is unemployed, is a successful lawyer.
2 Samantha has passed her driving test. She doesn't like taking the bus.
   _____
3 Many people earn a lot of money. They work overtime.
   _____
4 Mark is her only son. He is only ten years old.
   _____
5 The Four Seasons Hotel is closing down. I stayed there for a week.
   _____
6 The book is on the table. I have been looking for it.
   _____
7 Last summer was a wonderful time for me. The weather was hot then.
   _____
8 She avoided telling me the truth. I really can't explain it.
   _____

6 Complete the spaces in a–f with the correct pronoun. Then match with 1–6 to make sentences.

1 An employee is a person
2 A library is a building
3 An orphan is a child
4 A microscope is an instrument
5 2001 was the year
6 A pilot is a person

a _____ books are stored.
b _____ makes tiny things look bigger.
c _____ New York was attacked.
d _____ is paid to work for a company.
e _____ parents are dead.
f _____ flies a plane.

7 Complete the second sentence so that it has a similar meaning to the first sentence. Use the word in bold.

1 I met my wife in this place.
   where
   This _____ I met my wife.

2 That girl's father is in prison.
   whose
   That's _____ is in prison.

3 We ate a delicious meal last night.
   that
   The meal _____ was delicious.

4 I got a new laptop for my last birthday.
   when
   My last birthday _____ I got a new laptop.

5 He lost because he didn't train hard enough.
   why
   Not training hard enough _____ he lost.

6 The kidnapper escaped last week, but was arrested again yesterday.
   who
   Yesterday they arrested _____ last week.

Vocabulary

Phrasal verbs

8 Match the phrasal verbs with their meanings.

1 cut down on
2 keep away
3 keep to
4 keep up
5 fill in
6 fill up
7 hold down
8 get down to

a to stay far from, or stop someone from going near to something
b to keep a job
c to reduce the number or amount of something
d to start doing something properly
e to continue
f to complete a form
g to stick with a plan
h to make full

9 Complete the sentences with the correct form of the phrasal verbs from 8.

1 My uncle Tim was never able to _____ a job for long because he was always late!
2 Please _____ this form and return it to the office as soon as possible.
3 _____ the children _____ from the edge of the river – they can't swim.
4 I think it's time we really _____ work on this project.
5 Samantha is on a diet, so she's trying to _____ the amount of chocolate she eats every day.
6 _____ my glass to the top, please. I'm very thirsty.
7 I'm trying to _____ our original plan, but it's quite difficult because some things have to be changed.
8 You're doing a great job – _____ the good work!

Unit 17

Prepositions

10 Circle the correct words.

1. The city had been **over / through / under** attack for three days.
2. After the party, there were paper plates of half-eaten food all **over / through / under** the house.
3. The customs officer quickly glanced **over / through / under** my papers and then waved me on to the plane.
4. What time do you plan to pop **over / through / under** to Doug's place this evening?
5. Do not worry. I have the situation **over / through / under** control.
6. Let me **over / through / under**! I'm a doctor.

Collocations & Expressions

11 Complete the sentences with the correct form of **get**, **make** or **take**.

1. If you don't stop horsing around in the office, you'll _____ the sack.
2. He finally decided to _____ the initiative and phone his boss.
3. My dad's company _____ a huge profit last year.
4. Sarah has never _____ a day off the whole time she has worked here.
5. Let's just try to _____ the best of a bad situation.
6. You're never going to _____ rich if you have so much trouble getting out of bed.

Words easily confused

12 Use the words or phrase given to complete the sentences underneath. Make sure the words are in the correct form. Use each word or phrase at least once.

1. **allowance   pass   permission   permit**
   a. A _____ to fish this stretch of the river will cost you £150 a year.
   b. My father gives me a weekly _____ which I use to buy food and clothes.
   c. The headmaster gave us _____ to leave school early.
   d. Please wear your _____ so that the security personnel can see it easily.

2. **limp   stroll   tiptoe   wander**
   a. She loves _____ through the park on her way home from work every evening.
   b. It was three hours before our flight was scheduled, so we _____ aimlessly around the airport until it was time to go.
   c. I _____ into the nursery so that I wouldn't wake the baby.
   d. He had to _____ off the field with a leg injury.

3. **damp   humid   mild   wet**
   a. Where have you been? You're _____ through.
   b. We'd been expecting lots of snow but it turned out to be a _____ winter.
   c. Having lived in the tropics, he's used to a _____ climate.
   d. The old cottage is _____ inside because it has been empty for a year.

4. **fit   go with   match   suit**
   a. Red _____ both black and white.
   b. If the pullover doesn't _____, you can exchange it for a larger size.
   c. Jeans don't really _____ him – he looks much better in a suit.
   d. After buying a necklace, she searched for a pair of earrings to _____.

Word formation — prefixes

13 Use the word in capitals to form a word that fits in the gap.

1. There must be some kind of _____ – we didn't order any champagne. **UNDERSTAND**
2. Where did you _____ to last night? We looked everywhere for you. **APPEAR**
3. Try not to be so _____ – the bus will get here eventually. **PATIENT**
4. That was the most _____ magic trick I have ever seen. **CREDIBLE**
5. It took decades to _____ the city after it had been almost completely destroyed in the war. **BUILD**
6. Simon has been _____ ever since losing his job at the factory five years ago. **EMPLOY**
7. I have arranged to _____ the loan starting with £100 per month. **PAY**
8. In spite of his mother's _____, Mario bought a small motorcycle with his birthday money. **APPROVE**

Sentence transformation

14 Complete the second sentence so that it has a similar meaning to the first sentence, using the word given. Do not change the word given. You must use between two and five words.

1. I saw my first football match in this stadium.
   where
   This is _____ my first football match.

2. She saw her favourite film of all time yesterday.
   was
   The film _____ her favourite of all time.

3. You didn't get the job because you dressed too informally.
   reason
   The _____ get the job was because you dressed too informally.

4. That dog's owner is a police officer.
   whose
   That's _____ is a police officer.

5. 'Try to reduce the number of cigarettes you smoke', the doctor advised.
   down
   The doctor advised him _____ the number of cigarettes he smoked.

6. I'm going to start work on my novel properly this summer.
   get
   This summer, I'm _____ work on my novel.

7. They dismissed him from his last job.
   sack
   He _____ from his last job.

8. I'm sure I'm going to make a lot of money one day.
   get
   I'm sure that one day _____ rich.

Unit 18

Awareness

1 Which of these sentences are correct (C) and incorrect (I)?

1. I found the boy hiding behind the sofa. ___
2. The girl was awarded first prize started to cry. ___
3. Having saw the film before, I didn't go with my friends to the cinema. ___
4. Walking home last night, my phone's battery went dead. ___
5. Not knowing what to do, I emailed my mum. ___
6. Seen from a distance, the insect looked like a leaf. ___
7. Looked through the window, I saw something move. ___
8. The man speaks at the moment is my uncle. ___
9. Having had a long holiday, my desk was piled with paper. ___
10. Having chosen the colours for her room, she went out to buy the paint. ___

How many did you get right? ☐

Grammar
Participle clauses

There are two kinds of participles. The present participle (verb + *-ing*) and the past participle (verb + *-ed* or irregular form).

We can use participles in participle clauses to make sentences shorter. They can replace the subject and the verb in a sentence if the subject of both clauses is the same. We use a present participle if the verb is active and a past participle if the verb is passive.
*Before **starting** the course, Natalie had to buy a lot of text books.*
***Asked** if she would help organise the party, Tonya said that she was too busy.*

We can also use a participle to replace a relative pronoun and verb.
*The students **who were given** the awards were very happy.*
*The students **given** the awards were very happy.*
*The boy **who wanted to leave** the room put his hand up.*
*The boy **wanting** to leave the room put his hand up.*

We can also use a perfect participle (*having* + past participle) to combine clauses that have the same subject
• when one action is completed before another action.
***He polished** his car and drove down to the shopping mall.*
***Having polished** his car, he drove down to the shopping mall.*
• when one action has been going on for a period of time before another action starts.
***She had been sitting** in the sun for so long that she had turned bright red.*
***Having sat** in the sun for so long, she had turned bright red.*

The perfect participle can be used for active and passive voice.
• active voice: *having* + past participle (***Having slept** well, he felt refreshed.*)
• passive voice: *having been* + past participle (***Having been chosen** to compete, he began his preparations.*)

Grammar Exercises

2 Circle the correct words.
1 **Reading / Read** the newspaper that morning, Benny learned that his friend was in jail.
2 **Having spoken / After spoken** to her teacher, she applied to the local university.
3 Students **wishing / wished** to take part in the event must put their names down before the end of the week.
4 I'm interested in buying the car **advertising / advertised** on your web page.
5 **Not being / Not been** able to speak German, I asked Rudi to translate for me.
6 The woman **dancing / who dancing** on the table is my aunt Agatha.

3 Complete the sentences with the correct form of these verbs.

call   live   offer   send   steal   study

1 A lot of the artwork _____ in to our studio last week was excellent.
2 She was delighted when she received a letter _____ her a place at university.
3 Police are looking for a car _____ from the police car park last night.
4 A flood warning has been sent out to people _____ near the river.
5 A boy _____ Jacob is looking for you.
6 Every pupil _____ languages in this school has the opportunity to spend a month abroad.

4 Rewrite the sentences using a present participle clause.
1 Because I knew the traffic would be bad, I went by train.

2 I don't believe in ghosts, so I'm not scared of sleeping in castles.

3 While Christine was walking through the park, she thought about life in France.

4 Because we didn't want to disturb anyone, we tiptoed upstairs to bed.

5 I thought the dog might be hungry, so I gave it one of my sandwiches.

6 She didn't know David's phone number, so she couldn't contact him.

5 Rewrite the sentences using a past participle clause.
1 This song, which was written in the 1960s, remains one of the band's most popular.

2 The politician didn't know what to say when he was asked about the economy.

3 I would have been able to finish the exam if I had been given more time.

4 The man who was wanted by the police got on a plane to Brazil.

5 People all over the world admired Justin, but he didn't really like being famous.

6 The cat felt safe and happy because it was hidden under a pile of cushions.

Unit 18 123

Unit 18

6 Rewrite the sentences using a perfect participle clause.

1 As he had had a long holiday, Gerry felt quite refreshed.
___
2 After we had made the arrangements for the party, we had lunch.
___
3 Since I hadn't seen the film, I couldn't comment on it.
___
4 After you have decided where you want to go, you can buy the tickets here.
___
5 Because he hadn't had a bath for a couple of days, he felt dirty.
___
6 As we had heard the news already, we weren't taken by surprise.
___

Vocabulary

Phrasal verbs

7 Match the phrasal verbs with their meanings.

1 move in
2 move on
3 move out
4 take down
5 take on
6 take out
7 take round
8 take up

a to start something new
b to employ staff
c to begin living in a new house or flat
d to remove money from your bank account
e to leave the house or flat where you live
f to remove something from the wall
g to walk around a place with somebody to show it to them
h to fill an amount of time or space

8 Complete the sentences with the correct form of the phrasal verbs from 7.

1 Redecorating the baby's room _____ the whole weekend.
2 She's been working here for too long, and now thinks it's time to _____.
3 I think you should _____ that picture _____ – I've never liked it.
4 The paint factory is _____ extra staff during the summer.
5 Sonja, will you _____ the new student _____ the school today, please?
6 How much money did you _____ this morning?
7 We're _____ to our new flat this weekend.
8 Have the Jenkins _____ of their old house yet?

Prepositions

9 Circle the correct words.

1 Do not forget to sign the guest book **throughout / towards / upon** arrival.
2 Daniella still feels a lot of anger **throughout / towards / upon** her ex-boyfriend.
3 The night was ruined for me because the gentleman sitting next to us coughed **throughout / towards / upon** the show.
4 The new teacher has a strange attitude **throughout / towards / upon** her students.
5 When she came back into the room she had a big smile **throughout / towards / upon** her face.
6 It rained **throughout / towards / upon** the entire holiday.

Collocations & Expressions

10 Complete the sentences with these words.

> back books donkey feet monkey rat

1 If you can think on your _____, you can make decisions quickly when under pressure.
2 When there is _____ business going on, somebody is trying to trick you.
3 The _____ race is what we call life in the competitive world of business.
4 If you break your _____ doing something, it means that you work very hard at it.
5 When somebody cooks the _____, they are illegally changing the company's accounts to make money for themselves.
6 _____ work is work which is boring, repetitive and tiring.

Words easily confused

11 Use the words given to complete the sentences underneath. Make sure the words are in the correct form. Use each word at least once.

1 > current draught drought flood

  a There's a _____ in here. Please close the window.
  b Strong _____ make swimming here very dangerous.
  c _____ have become common after heavy rain.
  d _____ is always a problem in areas of little rainfall.

2 > claw hoof paw talon

  a The cat sank its _____ into my hand and ran away.
  b My dog was limping because it had a thorn stuck in its _____.
  c It was the unmistakable sound of a horse's _____.
  d An eagle's _____ are very strong indeed.

3 > demand inform instruct order

  a I wasn't _____ about any change in the timetable.
  b Who _____ a ham and mushroom pizza?
  c All employees will be _____ in the art of self-defence.
  d The customer _____ to speak to the manager in person.
  e Whoever _____ the soldiers to attack made a terrible mistake.

4 > agenda calendar catalogue directory list

  a Have you included Liam on the guest _____?
  b Look up her telephone number in the _____.
  c There's a _____ hanging on the kitchen wall.
  d As this item is not on the _____, we can't discuss it at this meeting.
  e He does most of his shopping through a mail order _____.

Word formation mixed

12 Use the word in capitals to form a word that fits in the gap.

1 Thank you for the _____ time we spent at your home. **WONDER**
2 We stayed in all morning waiting for a _____ that never came. **DELIVER**
3 It is a(n) _____ to be short if you are a basketball player. **ADVANTAGE**
4 It's much too _____ to drive. Let's stop until it clears up. **FOG**
5 I'll be happy with your decision because I trust your _____. **JUDGE**
6 My aunt and uncle have a very good _____ – they hardly ever argue. **RELATE**
7 Nobody talks to him because he has a reputation for being really _____. **FRIEND**
8 Barry is going to have to do something about his _____ if he wants to be a success in life. **LAZY**

Unit 18

Sentence transformation

13 Complete the second sentence so that it has a similar meaning to the first sentence, using the word given. Do not change the word given. You must use between two and five words.

1 I hate travelling by boat because I can't swim.
   able
   Not _____, I hate travelling by boat.

2 We bought some more oil because we had used it all.
   the
   Having _____, we bought some more.

3 It's time we employed more people to help us.
   took
   It's time _____ people to help us.

4 Will you show Luke the new building?
   round
   Will you _____ the new building?

5 Anna is very good at making decisions under pressure.
   feet
   Thinking _____ is something that Anna is very good at.

6 As soon as you arrive at the resort, you must pay the bill.
   upon
   You must pay the bill _____ the resort.

Unit 19

Awareness

1 Which of these sentences are correct (C) and incorrect (I)?

1. Tom told that he wouldn't be back before noon. ___
2. The head teacher told us that he had already made his decision. ___
3. She said that she had to go to bed early that night. ___
4. He asked me where did I live. ___
5. I told him that he had to look for a better job. ___
6. Mark said us that he had forgotten to book a table. ___
7. She told him to not go out of the house. ___
8. Sally told us that she had already paid the bill. ___
9. He asked me to stop. ___
10. Ian told that he didn't want me to help him. ___

How many did you get right? ☐

Grammar

Reported Speech: statements

When we report direct speech, the tenses used by the speaker usually change as follows.

Present Simple	**Past Simple**
'He **enjoys** reading,' she said.	She said (that) he **enjoyed** reading.
Present Continuous	**Past Continuous**
'She **is studying** physics,' he said.	He said (that) she **was studying** physics.
Present Perfect Simple	**Past Perfect Simple**
'They **have failed** their exams,' she said.	She said (that) they **had failed** their exams.
Present Perfect Continuous	**Past Perfect Continuous**
'They **have been looking** for CDs,' she said.	She said (that) they **had been looking** for CDs.
Past Simple	**Past Perfect Simple**
'She **went** to a meeting,' he said.	He said (that) she **had gone** to a meeting.
Past Continuous	**Past Perfect Continuous**
'He **was surfing** the Internet,' she said.	She said (that) he **had been surfing** the Internet.

Other changes in verb forms are as follows:

can	**could**
'He **can** speak five languages,' she said.	She said (that) he **could** speak five languages.
may	**might**
'He **may** be early,' she said.	She said (that) he **might** be early.
must	**had to**
'He **must** do his homework,' she said.	She said (that) he **had to** do his homework.
will	**would**
'They **will** go to Spain,' she said.	She said (that) they **would** go to Spain.

Unit 19

> **Note**
>
> **1** We often use the verbs *say* and *tell* in reported speech. We follow *tell* with an object.
> *My doctor **said** I should exercise more.*
> *My doctor **told me** that I should exercise more.*
>
> **2** We can leave out *that*.
> ***He said that** he preferred maths.* → ***He said** he preferred maths.*
>
> **3** Remember to change pronouns and possessive adjectives where necessary.
> '***We** are listening to music,'* he said. → *He said (that) **they** were listening to music.*
> '*That's **my** computer,'* **she** said. → *She said (that) that was **her** computer.*
>
> **4** The following tenses and words don't change in Reported Speech: Past Perfect Simple, Past Perfect Continuous, *would, could, might, should, ought to, used to, had better, mustn't* and *must* when they refer to deduction.

Reported Speech: Changes in time and place

When we report direct speech, there are often changes in words that show time and place too.

now	then
'I'm reading **now**,' she said.	She said she was reading **then**.
today	that day
'They're going away **today**,' he said.	He said they were going away **that day**.
tonight	that night
'I want to go out **tonight**,' she said.	She said she wanted to go out **that night**.
yesterday	the previous day / the day before
'I was ill **yesterday**,' he said.	He said he had been ill **the previous day / the day before**.
last week/month	the previous week/month / the week/month before
'He left school **last month**,' she said.	She said he had left school **the previous month / the month before**.
tomorrow	the next day / the following day
'We'll go to the beach **tomorrow**,' she said.	She said they would go to the beach **the next day / the following day**.
next week/month	the following week/month
'I'm starting karate lessons **next week**,' she said.	She said she was starting karate lessons **the following week**.
this/these	that/those
'**This** is my home town,' she said.	She said **that** was her home town.
ago	before
'The Olympics started two weeks **ago**,' she said.	She said the Olympics had started two weeks **before**.
at the moment	at that moment
'He's sleeping **at the moment**,' she said.	She said he was sleeping **at that moment**.
here	there
'The kids are **here** in the front room,' he said.	He said the kids were **there** in the front room.

Reported Speech: Questions

When we report questions, changes in tenses, pronouns, possessive adjectives, time and place are the same as in reported statements. In reported questions, the verb follows the subject as in ordinary statements and we do not use question marks.

When a direct question has a question word, we use this word in the reported question.
'**When** did you decide to study Chinese?' he asked.
He asked **when** I had decided to study Chinese.

When a direct question does not have a question word, we use *if* or *whether* in the reported question.
'Is your mother at home?' he asked.
He asked **if/whether** my mother was at home.

Reported Speech: Commands & Requests

When we report commands, we usually use *tell* + object + full infinitive.
'Turn off the TV!' he shouted at me.
He **told me to turn off** the TV.
'Don't forget your homework,' he said to the students.
He **told the students not to forget** their homework.

When we report a request, we usually use *ask* + object + full infinitive.
'Can you help me fix my bike, please?' she asked.
She **asked me to help** her fix her bike.
(Also: *She asked if I could help her fix her bike.*)
'Please don't shout at me,' she said.
She **asked me not to shout** at her.

Grammar Exercises

2 Complete the sentences with the correct form of **say** or **tell**.
1. She didn't _____ me that she would be late.
2. He _____ that it was Mary's fault.
3. Tom _____ so many lies that nobody believes him any more.
4. Sam _____ to me, 'I wasn't accepted by that college.'
5. He didn't _____ anything before he left.
6. Mary _____ Tom about the letter.

3 Choose the reported statement that means the same as the direct statement.
1. 'I got a job on an oil rig,' said Steven.
   a Steven said that he has got a job on an oil rig.
   b Steven said that he had got a job on an oil rig.
2. 'I can't afford to go out again,' Sally said to me.
   a Sally said me that she couldn't afford to go out again.
   b Sally told me that she couldn't afford to go out again.
3. 'I must do my homework now,' said the little boy.
   a The little boy said that he must do his homework then.
   b The little boy said that he had to do his homework then.
4. 'You broke the vase on purpose,' said Grandma.
   a Grandma said that I broken the vase on purpose.
   b Grandma said that I had broken the vase on purpose.
5. He said to me, 'You spend a lot of money on clothes.'
   a He told me that I spent a lot of money on clothes.
   b He told me that I had spent a lot of money on clothes.
6. He said, 'She has been listening to music for two hours.'
   a He said that she had been listening to music for two hours.
   b He said that she was listening to music for two hours.

Unit 19

4 Complete the sentences with the word that best fits each gap.

1. 'I want to see your brother this afternoon,' I said to her.
   I told her that I _____ to see her brother _____ afternoon.

2. 'I've missed the train; I'll be late for work,' said Betty.
   Betty said that she _____ the train and she _____ be late for work.

3. Alice said, 'My teacher made me rewrite my composition yesterday.'
   Alice said that her teacher _____ her rewrite her composition the day _____.

4. Mrs Brown said to me, 'I am waiting for my daughter at the moment.'
   Mrs Brown told me that she _____ for _____ daughter at _____ moment.

5. Bill said to Jane, 'I would like to take you out for dinner tomorrow.'
   Bill told Jane that he would like to take _____ out for dinner the _____ day.

6. John said to Sally, 'I've brought this for your birthday.'
   John told Sally that _____ had brought _____ for her birthday.

7. Carol said to him, 'I need you to help me carry some bags.'
   Carol told _____ that _____ needed _____ to help _____ carry some bags.

8. My mother said to my sister, 'You have to go to the supermarket this evening.'
   My mother told my sister that _____ had to go to the supermarket _____ evening.

5 Rewrite the sentences in reported speech.

1. His mother said to us, 'He has been talking on the phone for an hour.'
   _____

2. Ben said to his girlfriend, 'I really don't want to go to the cinema tonight.'
   _____

3. 'I am trying to concentrate on my work now,' said John.
   _____

4. 'He can't afford to buy a new house,' his mother said.
   _____

5. Her brother said to us, 'She'll come to your house when she has finished her homework.'
   _____

6. 'I haven't spoken to Jill since last month,' said Fiona.
   _____

7. His mother said to him, 'You must do your homework tonight.'
   _____

8. 'I met an old friend of mine two days ago,' said Emily.
   _____

6 Complete the reported questions so that they mean the same as the direct questions.

1 'When did Mr Brown leave the club?' asked the inspector.
The inspector asked _____.

2 'Where's the tin opener, George?' asked Yvonne.
Yvonne asked George _____.

3 'What do you think happened?' enquired Erica.
Erica asked me _____.

4 'Are you having a party on your birthday, Harry?' asked Tom.
Tom asked Harry _____.

5 'Do you have change for a £10 note?' he asked me.
He wanted to know _____.

6 'Why do you want to work for us?' asked the interviewer.
The interviewer asked me _____.

7 Rewrite the commands and requests in reported speech.

1 'Please don't mention this again,' he said to me.

2 'Don't bite your nails,' she said to him.

3 'Drink all your milk,' she said to her.

4 'Stop complaining, please,' he said to me.

5 'Don't lend Mary any money,' she said to me.

6 'Don't be rude to our guests,' he said to me.

7 'Tidy up your room, please,' she said to him.

8 'Please follow me,' the guide said to us.

Vocabulary

Phrasal verbs

8 Match the phrasal verbs with their meanings.

1 breeze through
2 brush up
3 drop out
4 fall through
5 figure out
6 go through
7 miss out on
8 run out

a to quit a course of study
b to improve a skill
c to succeed easily
d to understand something
e to fail to happen
f (of a supply) to completely finish or be used up
g to not do something which you would have enjoyed or benefited from
h to experience something difficult or unpleasant

Unit 19 **131**

Unit 19

9 Complete the sentences with the correct form of the phrasal verbs from 8.

1 Maria is _____ a difficult time at the moment.
2 He is so clever that he _____ every exam he takes.
3 Because of her illness, she _____ a lot of important lessons that term.
4 Bill _____ of university to start his own business.
5 I finally _____ how to programme this video recorder.
6 The tournament is next week, so you've only got five days to _____ your tennis skills.
7 We've _____ of petrol, and there is no garage for miles around.
8 I'm afraid the trip to London has _____ because I couldn't get the day off work.

Prepositions

10 Circle the correct words.

1 The police officer wouldn't help me because he said he was **from / off / over** duty.
2 We had a great holiday on an island **from / off / over** the coast of Italy.
3 Soon, the funny video was all **from / off / over** the Internet.
4 Who knows what we'll be doing five years **from / off / over** now?
5 They spoke **from / off / over** the intercom for a while, then she let him in.
6 I like to go on a long walk in the woods **from / off / over** time to time.

Collocations & Expressions

11 Match the two halves of the sentences to make definitions.

1 When you say you are brain dead ☐
2 A brainwave is ☐
3 If you pick someone's brains ☐
4 The brains behind something ☐
5 If you have something on your brain ☐
6 When you rack your brains ☐

a you think about it all the time.
b is the person who had the idea.
c you ask for their expert advice.
d you think very hard.
e a sudden, unexpected idea.
f you mean that you are too tired to think.

Words easily confused

12 Use the words given to complete the sentences underneath. Make sure the words are in the correct form. Use each word at least once.

1 **bank   border   boundary**
   a Thousands of refugees have crossed the _____ since fighting began.
   b This wall marks the _____ between our property and theirs.
   c As a teenager, he spent hours fishing from the _____ of the river.

2 **danger   emergency   risk   urgency**
   a According to Pat, it was a matter of some _____.
   b You can only use the phone in a(n) _____.
   c Several employees are in _____ of losing their jobs.
   d Don't take _____ if you can avoid it.
   e A general should never put his soldiers' lives at _____.

3 **bunch   bundle   collection   packet**
   a I always have a small _____ of grapes after lunch in summer.
   b She has a fine _____ of antique silver cups.
   c The tramp wandered the streets with his possessions tied in a _____.
   d I'll take a _____ of flowers when I visit them.
   e He threw his _____ of cigarettes away, promising never to smoke again.

4 | decrease drop lessen lower |

  a Please _____ your voice.
  b Take some extra blankets in case the temperature _____ below zero.
  c They put more police on the street to try to _____ the number of crimes in the area.
  d He wears a special belt to _____ the strain on his back.

Word formation mixed

13 Use the word in capitals to form a word that fits in the gap.

  1 It's a lovely old car, but it costs us a fortune in _____. **MAINTAIN**
  2 This is one of the _____ puzzles I have ever done in my life. **TRICK**
  3 The doctor suggested that a week's holiday would be _____ for me. **BENEFIT**
  4 You are not allowed in that restaurant if you are not _____ dressed. **SUIT**
  5 It's really _____ when you shout at the children like that – it only makes things worse. **HELP**
  6 Penicillin was the most important medical _____ of the 20th century. **DISCOVER**
  7 We were amazed at the hotel staffs' wonderful _____ to do whatever we asked. **WILL**
  8 Sam's mother is a famous _____. **NOVEL**

Sentence transformation

14 Complete the second sentence so that it has a similar meaning to the first sentence, using the word given. Do not change the word given. You must use between two and five words.

  1 'Please don't park here,' she said to me.
     asked
     She _____ park there.
  2 He told the children not to run.
     not
     'Do _____,' he told the children.
  3 'Where do you want to go this evening?' he asked us.
     that
     He asked us where _____ evening.
  4 Our teacher told us to listen to him.
     me
     '_____!' our teacher told us.
  5 'I can help you fix that,' she said.
     me
     She told me that she _____ fix that.
  6 'Do you want to go to university?' the professor asked them.
     if
     The professor asked _____ to go to university.
  7 'I'm busy at the moment,' she said.
     was
     She said she _____ moment.

Unit 19 133

Unit 20

Awareness

1 Which of these sentences are correct (C) and incorrect (I)?

1. Thank you for agreeing help us. ___
2. I advise you not to spend all your money. ___
3. She reminded me buying some tomatoes. ___
4. He recommends to put it in the oven for 50 minutes. ___
5. I apologise for being so thoughtless. ___
6. The teacher accused him of copying from the Internet. ___
7. She persuaded me go with her. ___
8. I promised taking them to the cinema. ___
9. They demanded that I bought them ice cream. ___
10. He was complaining about having to go to work so early. ___

How many did you get right? ☐

Grammar
Reported Speech: Reporting Verbs

Apart from the verbs *say*, *tell* and *ask*, we can also use other verbs to report what someone says more accurately.
Notice the different structures.

verb + full infinitive	
agree	'Yes, I'll fix it for you,' he said. He **agreed to fix** it for us.
claim	'I'm good at fixing things,' he said. He **claimed to be** good at fixing things.
decide	'I think I'll fix it,' he said. He **decided to fix** it.
refuse	'I won't fix it,' he said. He **refused to fix** it.
offer	'Shall I fix it?' he said. He **offered to fix** it.
promise	'Don't worry, I'll fix it,' he said. He **promised to fix** it.
verb + object + full infinitive	
advise	'If I were you, I'd exercise more,' he said. He **advised me to exercise** more.
encourage	'Go on, exercise more and you'll feel great,' he said. He **encouraged me to exercise** more.
order	'Exercise more!' he said. He **ordered me to exercise** more.
persuade	'You should exercise more – you'll feel great,' he said. 'You're right!' I said. He **persuaded me to exercise** more.
remind	'Don't forget to exercise,' he said. He **reminded me to exercise**.
warn	'Exercise more or you'll get fat,' he said. He **warned me to exercise** more.
verb + gerund (*-ing*)	
admit	'I lost the money,' he said. He **admitted losing** the money.
deny	'I didn't lose the money,' he said. He **denied losing** the money.
recommend	'You should keep it in a wallet,' he said. He **recommended keeping** it in a wallet.
suggest	'Let's buy a wallet,' he said. He **suggested buying** a wallet.
verb + preposition + gerund (*-ing*)	
apologise for	'I'm sorry I broke your laptop,' he said. He **apologised for breaking** my laptop.
complain of/about	'I broke my laptop again,' he said. He **complained about breaking** his laptop again.
insist on	'Don't be silly. I'll buy a new laptop for you,' he said. He **insisted on buying** a new laptop for me.

verb + object + preposition + gerund (-ing)	
accuse sb of	'I'm sure you stole my keys,' he said. He **accused me of stealing** his keys.
congratulate sb on	'You found your keys! Well done!' he said. He **congratulated me on finding** my keys.
verb + *that*	
announce	'I'm going to do it,' he said. He **announced that** he was going to do it.
complain	'I don't have time to do it,' he said. He **complained that** he didn't have time to do it.
demand	'You do it,' he said. He **demanded that** I do it.

Grammar Exercises

2 Circle the correct words.
1. Sandra **agreed / insisted** to cook dinner.
2. The head teacher **advised / suggested** me to apply to university.
3. The boy **apologised / admitted** breaking the window.
4. He **complained / refused** that he was hungry.
5. My dad **congratulated / encouraged** me on winning the race.
6. I'm surprised that he **denied / refused** to sign the papers.
7. The policeman **persuaded / demanded** them to go home quietly.
8. He **claimed / admitted** to be a great tennis player.
9. I **accused / warned** my classmate of copying my work.
10. My sister **offered / reminded** me to go to the shops.

3 Complete the sentences with the correct form of the verbs in brackets.
1. She suggested _____ (eat) at the new restaurant.
2. The man denied _____ (steal) the money.
3. I was so glad that Simon agreed _____ (come) with us.
4. My trainer encouraged me _____ (enter) the competition.
5. Donna demanded that I _____ (drive) her back to her house.
6. He claimed _____ (be) the president's cousin.
7. She complained that she _____ (not have) time to clean the house.
8. I apologised for _____ (not remember) my sister's birthday.

4 Complete the sentences in reported speech using an appropriate reporting verb.
1. 'You took my car and crashed it,' he said to me.
   He _____.
2. 'You should eat less fatty food,' said the doctor.
   The doctor _____.
3. 'Don't forget to bring the things I asked for,' she said to me.
   She _____.
4. 'I'm so sorry I damaged the bike,' the child said.
   The child _____.
5. 'You hit John with your bag,' said the teacher to Kevin.
   The teacher _____.
6. 'Leave the courtroom immediately,' the judge said to the jury.
   The judge _____.
7. She said to me, 'If I were you, I would consult a lawyer.'
   She _____.
8. 'Please don't be angry with me,' she said to her father.
   She _____.

Unit 20

5 Complete the sentences with the word that best fits each gap.
1 He decided _____ move to Italy.
2 She advised _____ not to buy it, so I didn't.
3 I don't believe he accused you _____ lying.
4 What was she apologising _____? It wasn't her fault!
5 My dad insisted _____ paying the bill.
6 The teacher announced _____ there was going to be a test the next day.

6 Change the reported speech into direct speech.
1 Karl ordered Ben to go to bed, but Ben refused.
   Karl: *Go to bed.*
   Ben: *No, I won't.*
2 The twins asked Glenda to help them. Glenda agreed.
   Twins: _____
   Glenda: _____
3 Sara accused Tom of eating her sandwich. Tom denied it.
   Sara: _____
   Tom: _____
4 Mum reminded me to buy a present for Greg. I thanked her.
   Mum: _____
   Me: _____
5 The doctor advised me to drink more water, and I agreed.
   Doctor: _____
   Me: _____
6 The policeman ordered the boy to get off his bike. The boy refused.
   Policeman: _____
   Boy: _____

Vocabulary

Phrasal verbs

7 Match the phrasal verbs with their meanings.

1 go for ☐   a to learn by practising
2 go over ☐   b to try to get
3 hand in ☐   c to look at again, revise
4 hand out ☐   d to submit work
5 look out for ☐   e to find something in a list of things
6 look up ☐   f to unfairly criticize or badly treat one person
7 pick on ☐   g to distribute something among a group
8 pick up ☐   h to try to notice something or somebody

8 Complete the sentences with the correct form of the phrasal verbs from 7.
1 Sam _____ quite of lot of Spanish, even though he lived there for only four months.
2 _____ Gina when you go to the conference. She said she was going.
3 I'm training very hard because this time I am _____ the gold medal.
4 You shouldn't _____ Tim – he needs to be encouraged, not criticized.
5 If you don't know what I'm talking about, _____ it _____ on *Google*.
6 He _____ the vocabulary list one more time before doing the test.
7 Your homework will not be marked if you _____ it _____ late.
8 The teacher _____ the worksheets to everyone in the class.

Prepositions

9 Circle the correct words.

1. It's **against / after / along** the law to drive without a seatbelt on.
2. We never invited John to our house again **against / after / along** the way he behaved.
3. What do your parents think about having a TV in your bedroom? Mine are **against / after / along** it.
4. There were lots of little cafés and shops **against / after / along** the road.
5. I knew all **against / after / along** that Stefan was not an honest person.
6. It turned out that we were going in the right direction **against / after / along** all.

Collocations & Expressions

10 Complete the sentences with the correct form of **take**, **get** or **keep**.

1. Susan _____ great pleasure in baking cakes for birthday parties.
2. I _____ the feeling that Theresa is going to leave her job soon – she seems very unhappy.
3. Would you like me to _____ you company on the journey into town this afternoon?
4. Let me _____ straight to the point – I don't think you are working hard enough.
5. I didn't know the sports centre was open on Sunday, but I'll _____ your word for it.
6. Dad _____ his promise to me and bought me a bicycle for my birthday.

Words easily confused

11 Use the words given to complete the sentences underneath. Make sure the words are in the correct form. Use each word at least once.

1. **comment   mention   notice   refer**
   - a Please don't _____ the excursion to Howard – I didn't invite him.
   - b He didn't _____ on your work at all.
   - c I wish I hadn't _____ to my ambitions during the discussion.
   - d The robbery occurred so quickly that only one witness _____ what the robbers were wearing.

2. **nation   people   race   tribe**
   - a The human _____ is responsible for its own future.
   - b Some _____ just don't know how to behave!
   - c Several _____ have applied to become members of the UN.
   - d Probably the most famous Indian _____ is the Apache.

3. **cash   cheque   credit   installment**
   - a She never pays in _____.
   - b Your next _____ is due on 5th July.
   - c I don't have any money with me, so can I pay by _____?
   - d We accept all major _____ cards.

4. **only   separate   single   unique**
   - a Being a(n) _____ child, she had no brothers or sisters to play with.
   - b It's a(n) _____ opportunity for you to travel abroad.
   - c Are you married or _____?
   - d Remember to keep the letters from head office _____ from all the others.
   - e I'd rather have two _____ rooms than a double.

Unit 20

Word formation — mixed

12 Use the word in capitals to form a word that fits in the gap.

1 Unfortunately, we got lost in the old city because a policeman had given us _____ information. **LEAD**
2 It is not _____ to expect a small child to understand such a complex maths problem. **REASON**
3 I am writing in _____ to the recent documentary broadcast on your TV station. **REFER**
4 He is a very _____ boy, who is always doing something exciting. **ADVENTURE**
5 I'm afraid the situation is completely _____ – there is no way you can get your money back now. **HOPE**
6 Don't make any sudden _____ or you will frighten the birds. **MOVE**
7 Everyone was surprised when our team won the _____. **CHAMPION**
8 Greg was shocked at the _____ of the people he encountered at the convention – nobody spoke to him! **FRIENDLY**

Sentence transformation

13 Complete the second sentence so that it has a similar meaning to the first sentence, using the word given. Do not change the word given. You must use between two and five words.

1 'OK, I'll give you a lift to the concert,' said Tom.
   to
   Tom _____ us a lift to the concert.

2 'Sit down!' she said to us.
   ordered
   She _____ down.

3 'It's true, I crashed the car,' Becky said.
   admitted
   Becky _____ the car.

4 'I'm really sorry I hurt you,' he said to her.
   for
   He _____ her.

5 'Well done! You won the competition,' he said to me.
   on
   He _____ the competition.

6 'Tell me how you discovered my password!' she said to me.
   that
   She demanded _____ how I discovered her password.

7 'You lied to me,' she said.
   of
   She _____ to her.

8 'No, I won't do what you tell me,' he said to them.
   refused
   He _____ they told him.

Review 5

B2 Practice: FCE

Part 1

For questions 1–12, read the text below and decide which answer (A, B, C or D) best fits each gap. There is an example at the beginning (0).

Jailbirds

Although the therapeutic (0) __ of pets has been appreciated for some time, they have not been permitted in British prisons until relatively (1) __.

Not long ago it (2) __ to the prison authorities that prisoners serving long sentences must feel (3) __ by society and that was (4) __ the reason why they became less cooperative. It was then suggested that they were likely to respond positively if they were (5) __ to keep a budgie. Realising that long-term prisoners go through a great deal of suffering, the appropriate government department went (6) __ with the idea.

After a trial period, the authorities (7) __ the conclusion that looking after a small, helpless bird brought out a (8) __ side in most prisoners. This, in turn, (9) __ some prisoners and their jailers closer together. The authorities were relieved because there had been some (10) __ to the scheme who had passionately warned against it.

Since the scheme was set up, inmates have been able to (11) __ from the boredom of prison life and see their situation from a completely different (12) __.

0	A	price	B	cost	C	value	D	worth
1	A	lately	B	recently	C	shortly	D	soon
2	A	happened	B	considered	C	resulted	D	occurred
3	A	abandoned	B	vanished	C	mislaid	D	left
4	A	accurately	B	truly	C	precisely	D	likely
5	A	allowed	B	let	C	left	D	agreed
6	A	across	B	along	C	down	D	up
7	A	came	B	got	C	arrived	D	reached
8	A	sensitive	B	sensible	C	logical	D	truthful
9	A	fetched	B	took	C	brought	D	carried
10	A	rivals	B	opponents	C	counters	D	competitors
11	A	prevent	B	avoid	C	escape	D	block
12	A	corner	B	edge	C	angle	D	opinion

Review 5

Part 2

For questions 13–24, read the text below and think of the word which best fits each gap. Use only one word in each gap. There is an example at the beginning (0).

Gambling

In these days of high unemployment it might (0) __be__ expected that people would try to save as (13) _____ money as possible. However, the surprising fact is that people prefer gambling (14) _____ putting money aside during an economic depression.

Gambling takes (15) _____ forms and most people do it at one time or another. The majority bet small amounts on horse races, lotteries, or scratch cards. They probably regard it (16) _____ a kind of hobby which may improve the quality of their lives. Although they know very few (17) _____ been successful, they are (18) _____ hopeful that they will win a large sum of money that they carry on betting. Fortunately, this group usually knows (19) _____ to stop, so they can (20) _____ least control the amount they spend.

There are, on the other hand, those who have (21) _____ a strong desire to gamble that they ignore anyone who tries to stop them. They (22) _____ to bet in order to satisfy their addiction. These people will risk losing all their money. They (23) _____ rather lose their jobs or cause their marriage to break down (24) _____ give up gambling.

Part 3

For questions 25–34, read the text below. Use the word given in capitals at the end of each line to form a word that fits in the gap in the same line. There is an example at the beginning (0).

Taking the blame

Among many other things, (0) __pollution__ has become a sensitive	**POLLUTE**
political issue in many countries in the world today. All parties, not just the Greens,	
now include (25) _____ policies in their election manifestos.	**ENVIRONMENT**
As a result of this, one would be forgiven for assuming that the amount of	
(26) _____ waste being released is decreasing. However,	**INDUSTRY**
the evidence suggests that this is very unlikely to be the case. In fact, all the research	
to date shows that the (27) _____ of our environment is not	**DESTROY**
slowing down at all. It is a truly (28) _____ issue which requires	**GLOBE**
international cooperation to combat, and it appears that we are failing. Many	
attempts have been made to (29) _____ the reasons for this.	**IDENTITY**
It is easy to point the finger at (30) _____ government	**INFLUENCE**
ministers and businessmen, and it does appear that many of them are behaving	
(31) _____. But it could be argued that putting the blame on	**RESPONSIBLE**
these people (32) _____ gives the general public license	**SIMPLE**
to continue (33) _____ consuming the very products which	**GREEDY**
are causing such devastating damage to the environment. If the public's	
(34) _____ was more positive and well-informed, perhaps	**RESPOND**
the situation would change for the better.	

Part 4

For questions 35–42, complete the second sentence so that it has a similar meaning to the first sentence, using the word given. Do not change the word given. You must use between two and five words, including the word given. Here is an example (0).

Example:

0 It isn't necessary for you to go to every lesson.
attend
You _____ *needn't attend* _____ every lesson.

35 The president found what the manager said embarrassing.
embarrassed
The president _____ comments.

36 Her brother didn't have nearly as much success in the job as she did.
more
She did the job _____ her brother.

37 A famous architect is designing a house for them.
designed
They _____ by a famous architect.

38 He started his stamp collection about 20 years ago.
collecting
He _____ about 20 years.

39 You really shouldn't play on this court without permission.
supposed
You _____ on this court without permission.

40 I'd rather work here than get a job in the city.
prefer
I _____ a job in the city.

41 Tommy often forgets to switch on the alarm.
time
It's not the _____ to switch on the alarm.

42 You can buy two boxes for the price of one at this shop.
sale
Boxes are _____ price at this shop.

Review 5

B2 Practice: ECCE

Grammar

For questions 1–20 choose the word or phrase that best completes the sentence or conversation.

1. 'Where's Julia?'
   'She ___ that she'd be back soon.'
   A said
   B told
   C asked
   D talked

2. Mrs Smith, ___ I thought was on holiday, is here.
   A which
   B that
   C who
   D she

3. He apologised ___ being late.
   A for
   B to
   C of
   D with

4. The policeman ___ ride on the pavement.
   A told me to not
   B told me not to
   C said me not to
   D said me to not

5. The woman ___ at the moment is my mum.
   A speaking
   B speaks
   C to speak
   D speak

6. ___ being able to dance, I don't enjoy parties.
   A No
   B None
   C Not
   D Can't

7. ___ from the air, the patterns are quite beautiful.
   A Seeing
   B See
   C Saw
   D Seen

8. Not wanting ___ rude, I sat quietly until the end of the meal.
   A being
   B be
   C was
   D to be

9. Why did you insist ___ early?
   A to leave
   B on leaving
   C leaving
   D on leave

10. 'Did he ___ if you were okay?'
    'No, he just drove off!'
    A say
    B tell
    C ask
    D talk

11. Do you know the reason ___ it happened?
    A how
    B when
    C which
    D why

12. I asked her ___ she would like to have dinner.
    A whether
    B that
    C may
    D could

13. ___ heard the music, I didn't buy the CD.
    A Being
    B Having
    C Doing
    D Making

14. 'Where's Greta?'
    'She decided ___ at home.'
    A stay
    B staying
    C stayed
    D to stay

15. 'Why are you angry with him?'
    'He accused me ___!'
    A to cheat
    B of cheating
    C cheating
    D cheat

16. Our house, ___ we bought in 2010, is for sale.
    A which
    B what
    C who
    D it

17. 'Why didn't Dan want to eat anything?'
    'He said he ___ dinner.'
    A already has
    B had already
    C has already has
    D had already had

18. I recommend ___ to see this play.
    A to go
    B of going
    C going
    D go

19. 'Who is that?'
    'That's the girl ___ dad is the new head teacher.'
    A which
    B who's
    C that's
    D whose

20. This is ___ I sleep.
    A room
    B where
    C bed
    D place

Vocabulary

For questions 21–40, choose the word or phrase that most appropriately completes the sentence.

21 Could you ___ in this application form, please?
A put
B fill
C hold
D write

22 I knew who the murderer was all ___.
A against
B after
C along
D away

23 She ___ through her final exams easily.
A blew
B ran
C breezed
D whistled

24 Have you ___ out how to do it yet?
A numbered
B wondered
C calculated
D figured

25 How did he ___ so rich?
A be
B make
C take
D get

26 Playing computer games ___ up too much of your time.
A makes
B takes
C spends
D holds

27 Do you think you'll still be here five years ___ now?
A by
B from
C out
D away

28 We have lived here long enough. I think it's time to ___ out.
A go
B make
C move
D leave

29 I'll pop ___ to your house this evening.
A after
B under
C through
D over

30 The sun shone ___ the weekend.
A in
B throughout
C out
D within

31 I'm tired of doing all the ___ work for you.
A monkey
B dog
C horse
D donkey

32 He decided to leave the rat ___ and buy a small place in the country.
A race
B show
C event
D run

33 There is litter ___ over the place!
A every
B all
C some
D around

34 Keep ___ the good work, Jerry!
A up
B down
C on
D off

35 May I ___ your brains about this project?
A pick
B rack
C kick
D pack

36 I'm amazed at how quickly you ___ up the language.
A lifted
B got
C took
D picked

37 Look ___ for the traffic wardens around here!
A out
B up
C over
D along

38 Do you ever ___ the feeling that you're being watched?
A take
B make
C hold
D get

39 It was a boring journey with nobody to ___ me company.
A give
B hand
C keep
D bring

40 Oh no! We've run ___ of milk.
A out
B off
C over
D off

Unit 21

Awareness

1 Which of these sentences are correct (C) and incorrect (I)?

1. My new MP3 player is most expensive than yours. ___
2. Today is the hottest day of the year. ___
3. We arrived very lately at the party. ___
4. This cartoon isn't as funny as the last one. ___
5. The higher you climb, the more you can see. ___
6. You'll get there more quick if you cycle. ___
7. She gave the toy to the child who asked the most politely. ___
8. I'm much fitter that you. ___
9. This is the worst photography exhibition I've ever seen. ___
10. Jude is just as clever as his sister. ___

How many did you get right? ☐

Grammar
Comparison of Adjectives & Adverbs

We use the comparative to compare two people or things. We usually form the comparative by adding *-er* to an adjective or adverb. If the adjective or adverb has two or more syllables, we use the word *more*. We often use the word *than* after the comparative.
First class tickets are **more expensive than** second class tickets.
Class 3B plays **more noisily than** class 4B.

We use the superlative to compare one person or thing with other people or things of the same type. We usually form the superlative by adding *-est* to the adjective or adverb. If the adjective or adverb has two or more syllables, we use the word *most*. We use the word *the* before the superlative.
What is **the longest** river in the world?
Sara sang **the most beautifully**.

Spelling: ho**t** → ho**tter**/ho**ttest**, brav**e** → brav**er**/brav**est**, tin**y** → tin**ier**/tin**iest**.

Some adjectives and adverbs are irregular and form their comparative and superlative in different ways.

Adjective/Adverb	Comparative	Superlative
good/well	better	the best
bad/badly	worse	the worst
many/more	more	the most
much	more	the most
little	less	the least
far	farther/further	the farthest/furthest

> **Note**
> 1 Some words like *hard, late, straight* and *fast* are both adjectives and adverbs.
> 2 Other words like *friendly, lovely, silly,* and *ugly*, even though they end in *-ly* are not adverbs but adjectives.
> 3 The words *hardly* (= barely) and *lately* (= recently) are not the adverbs of *hard* and *late*.

Other comparative structures

We use *as* + adjective/adverb + *as* to show that two people or things are similar in some way.
*Do you think football is **as exciting as** basketball?*

We use *not as/so* + adjective/adverb + *as* to show that one person or thing has less of a quality than another.
*New York **isn't as polluted as** Los Angeles.*

We use *the* + comparative, *the* + comparative to show that as one thing increases or decreases, another thing is affected.
***The harder** he trained, **the better** he became.*

Grammar Exercises

2 Circle the correct words.
1. This is the **most easy / easiest** test I've ever done.
2. In fact, the test wasn't as **harder / hard** as I expected.
3. Al Pacino is one of the **more talented / most talented** actors of his generation.
4. Antonio can't speak English as **good / well** as Philip.
5. Our flight to Madrid took **the longest / longer** than we expected.
6. 'How are you today?' 'Well, I feel **more bad / worse** than yesterday.'
7. The Empire State Building was once **the taller / the tallest** building in the world.
8. He didn't answer the questions as **quickly / quick** as I did.

3 Complete the sentences with the comparative or superlative form of the adjectives in brackets.
1. Last night, I went to one of the _____ (good) concerts I have ever been to.
2. Living in the country is _____ (healthy) than living in a city.
3. Business Class is _____ (comfortable) than Economy.
4. Learning Chinese is _____ (difficult) than learning English.
5. Mrs Hamilton is _____ (strict) teacher in our school.
6. John is much _____ (naughty) than Peter.
7. This is _____ (delicious) food that I've ever eaten.
8. Tom is _____ (careful) than John. John always makes mistakes.
9. Another person got the job because he was much _____ (experienced) than me.
10. That's _____ (silly) thing I've ever heard!

4 Rewrite the sentences with *as ... as*.
1. Jill can walk faster than Mary.
   Mary can't _____.
2. My mother works harder than my father.
   My father doesn't _____.
3. Flying to New York takes more time than flying to Athens.
   Flying to Athens doesn't _____.
4. You have visited more places in England than I have.
   I haven't _____.
5. Shopping centres are more convenient than small shops.
   Small shops aren't _____.
6. James can drive faster than Timothy can.
   Timothy _____.

Unit 21 **145**

Unit 21

5 Use the prompts to write sentences.

1 I / run / fast / you

2 Gold / be / expensive / silver

3 James / drive / carefully / his brother

4 The North Pole / cold / place / the world

5 She / be / bad / singer / the school

6 Tony / be / naughty / boy / our class

7 This / be / good / restaurant / the city

8 Jerry / be / clever / Tom

9 Tim / not like / me / much / John

10 The Olympics / be / important sports event

6 Rewrite the sentences with the + comparative, the + comparative.

1 As she grew older, she became less patient.

2 You are more likely to have an accident when you drive fast.

3 If you work quickly, you'll be able to leave sooner.

4 As he went further into the forest, he became more frightened.

5 As I learnt more about the subject, it seemed to be more interesting.

6 As our cat got older, it got fatter.

7 Complete the sentences with the word that best fits each gap.

1 My sister doesn't cook _____ well as I do. In other words, I am much better _____ her.
2 You can't walk _____ fast _____ I can.
3 John is _____ youngest boy in the class.
4 Jane thinks she is cleverer _____ me.
5 The bigger your house is, _____ more furniture you need.
6 The test was less difficult _____ I expected.

Vocabulary

Phrasal verbs

8 Match the phrasal verbs with their meanings.

1. book into
2. break into
3. break out
4. check in
5. check out
6. check up on
7. pull in
8. work out

a to arrange for a room in a hotel
b to exercise
c to pay the bill and leave a hotel
d to drive your car off the road and into a place
e (of something unpleasant) to suddenly start
f to arrive and register at a hotel or airport
g to find out how somebody or something is progressing
h to illegally enter a building

9 Complete the sentences with the correct form of the phrasal verbs from 8.

1. The driver needed a break, so we _____ to a roadside café for a drink.
2. Somebody _____ the computer lab yesterday and stole the printer.
3. We always _____ a hotel close to the airport the night before we fly.
4. Fighting has _____ between rival football supporters in the centre of town.
5. Danny is _____ in the hotel gym at the moment.
6. Can you _____ grandma on your way to work? She hasn't been feeling well.
7. When we got to the airport, the first thing we did was _____.
8. We _____ of the hotel at 11 am and got a taxi to the station.

Prepositions

10 Circle the correct words.

1. Uncle Jim is **in / on / within** a luxury cruise around the Bahamas at the moment.
2. Is there a doctor **in / on / within** board the ship?
3. We travelled south **in / on / within** search of sun, sea and sand.
4. Fortunately, there was a chemist **in / on / within** walking distance of our hotel.
5. Our team came **in / on / within** five points of winning the match.
6. I really hate having to stand **in / on / within** line at airports.

Collocations & Expressions

11 Complete the sentences with these words.

| compartment | crew | excess | gate | in-flight | pass |

1. If you don't have a boarding _____, they won't let you on the plane.
2. Please put your hand luggage in the overhead _____.
3. I don't mind long plane journeys as long as there is plenty of _____ entertainment.
4. The cabin _____ on this plane are very friendly.
5. We bought so much stuff on holiday that we had to pay _____ baggage on the flight home.
6. Flight B341 to Berlin is ready for boarding at departure _____ 18.

Unit 21 **147**

Unit 21

Words easily confused

12 Use the words given to complete the sentences underneath. Make sure the words are in the correct form. Use each word at least once.

1. last   late   latest   latter   recent
   a She's the _____ person I expected to see at the reception.
   b _____ research suggests that time travel might be possible.
   c Brian and Barry both showed great ability but only the _____ won an Olympic medal.
   d His _____ film is set to become a blockbuster.
   e The _____ Dr Evans will be missed by family and friends alike.

2. combine   compare   join   share   stick
   a I'd like to _____ a secret with you.
   b We had better _____ together, or we might get lost.
   c It's far from easy for me to _____ work with leisure.
   d Please _____ the sweets I gave you with your cousin.
   e How do I go about _____ the club?

3. certificate   degree   licence   subject
   a History was the one _____ I was never good at.
   b I seem to have lost my birth _____.
   c She has a _____ in architecture from Birmingham University.
   d This driving _____ is not valid in Canada.

4. belong   own   possess
   a If it doesn't _____ to you, why is it in your bag?
   b His one ambition is to _____ a genuine Picasso.
   c For a person who _____ such skill, his work is often rather poor.

Word formation mixed

13 Use the word in capitals to form a word that fits in the gap.

1. _____ are responsible for most of the road accidents in this city. **MOTOR**
2. The children sang _____, and the acting was excellent. **DELIGHT**
3. We took a short cut through a _____ field. **MUD**
4. Everyone was impressed by the _____ of the circus master's dog. **INTELLIGENT**
5. Any painting by Da Vinci is _____ – nobody could afford one. **PRICE**
6. That was not a very good _____, considering how much they practised. **PERFORM**
7. My dad is a medical _____ at City Hospital. **CONSULT**
8. Our party will fight for liberty, freedom, and _____ for all. **EQUAL**

Sentence transformation

14 Complete the second sentence so that it has a similar meaning to the first sentence, using the word given. Do not change the word given. You must use between two and five words.

1 Philip and Ray are the same height.
   tall
   Philip _____ Ray.

2 Sirius is the brightest star of all.
   shines
   Sirius _____ any other star.

3 Hank plays better than anyone I know.
   as
   I don't know anyone _____ Hank.

4 It doesn't rain as much in Greece as it does in England.
   often
   It rains _____ it does in Greece.

5 Amsterdam is not nearly as far away as Tokyo.
   much
   Tokyo is _____ Amsterdam.

6 We could walk from the hotel to the beach.
   within
   The beach _____ of our hotel.

7 Can you make sure Ellie is ok when you go upstairs?
   up
   Can you _____ when you go upstairs?

8 Do you exercise very often when you are on holiday?
   work
   How often _____ when you are on holiday?

Unit 22

Awareness

1 Which of these sentences are correct (C) and incorrect (I)?

1 Your test results weren't enough good. ___
2 It was fairly freezing yesterday. ___
3 I am absolutely starving. ___
4 This soup is too hot. ___
5 That dress is such gorgeous. ___
6 That's a charming old necklace. ___
7 The weather was so bad we didn't leave our hotel. ___
8 Have you seen my white long trousers? ___
9 You're not driving fast enough. ___
10 I'm afraid your goldfish is extremely dead. ___

How many did you get right? ☐

Grammar

Too, Enough, So & Such

We use *too* + adjective/adverb to show that something is more than we want or need.
It's **too cold** to go swimming.
She was speaking **too quickly** for me to understand.

We use adjective/adverb + *enough* or *enough* + noun to show that something is or isn't as much as we want or need.
The cyclist wasn't riding **fast enough**.
I have **enough sandwiches** for everyone.

We use *so* and *such* for emphasis. It is stronger than *very*.
• We use *so* + adjective/adverb.
His bedroom was **so tidy**!
• We use *such* + (adjective) + noun.
The walls were painted **such a horrible colour**.

We can also use *so* and *such* to emphasise characteristics that lead to a certain result or action.
It was **such a great book** that I've read it four times!
The train carriage was **so cold** that there was ice on the windows.

Gradable Adjectives

Gradable adjectives can
• vary in intensity or grade.
It's **hot** today, but it was **very hot** yesterday.
• be used with grading adverbs such as *a little, extremely, fairly, hugely, immensely, intensely, rather, reasonably, slightly, unusually, very*, etc.
Our hotel was **fairly big**, but **reasonably cheap**.
• have comparative and superlative forms.
The ghost train was **more exciting** than the haunted house, but the roller coaster was the **most exciting** of all.

Non-gradable Adjectives

Non-gradable adjectives
• cannot vary in intensity or grade because they are already at their limit.
The water is **boiling**.
This parrot is **dead**.
• are often used alone.
It was **freezing** in the town square.
He was **late**, and she was **furious**.
• can only be used with non-grading adverbs such as *absolutely, utterly, completely, totally*, etc.
I'm **utterly starving**!
That meal was **absolutely perfect**.

> **Note**
> The adverbs *really, fairly, pretty* and *quite* can often be used with gradable and non-gradable adjectives.
> Jason is **pretty clever** for his age.
> The book was **pretty terrible**, wasn't it?

Adjective Order

When we use two or more adjectives to describe something or someone, we usually put them in the following order.

opinion	size	age	shape	colour	origin	material	
nice	small	old	round	pink	Parisian	cotton	NOUN
beautiful	large	new	oval	beige	Italian	wooden	
charming	big	ancient	long	white	Japanese	ceramic	

She lives in a **beautiful old English** cottage.
Tiny yellow plastic balls were scattered all over the floor.

Grammar Exercises

2 Circle the correct words.
1. My grandpa is **too / enough** old to drive.
2. The sea is warm **too / enough** to swim in.
3. The food is **too / enough** cold to eat.
4. Sheila is **too / enough** young to read.
5. She runs fast **too / enough** to win a medal.
6. I was **too / enough** angry to speak.
7. That house is big **too / enough** for us to live in.
8. Are you brave **too / enough** to jump off this wall?

3 Combine the sentences using *too* or *enough*.
1. That car is very expensive. I can't afford it.
   _____
2. Mike isn't tall. He can't join the police force.
   _____
3. This coffee is very sweet. I can't drink it.
   _____
4. I was very afraid. I couldn't open the door.
   _____
5. He wasn't quick. He couldn't catch the ball.
   _____
6. That exercise is very difficult. I can't do it.
   _____
7. Jim isn't rich. He can't buy a new house.
   _____
8. Jake is very clever. He can solve the puzzle.
   _____

Unit 22

4 Complete the sentences with so or such.
1 This is _____ a long book.
2 It was _____ terrible weather that the streets were empty.
3 She walks _____ slowly that everybody gets impatient with her.
4 You live in _____ a beautiful house.
5 The sea was _____ rough that the boat trip was cancelled.
6 Her brother is _____ handsome!
7 Yesterday was _____ a beautiful day.
8 Your taste in music is _____ awful, I can't stand it.

5 Complete the second sentence so that it has a similar meaning to the first sentence. Use the word in bold.
1 I can't reach it because I am too short.
   tall
   I _____ to reach it.
2 This bed is so uncomfortable.
   such
   This _____ bed.
3 Your sister is such an amazing dancer.
   so
   Your sister _____ amazingly.
4 How do you get your teeth so white?
   such
   How do you get _____ teeth?
5 You are not old enough to watch this film.
   young
   You _____ to watch this film.
6 That little boy is so badly behaved.
   such
   That is _____ little boy.

6 Complete the sentences with the adverb that best fits each gap.
1 That dessert was _____ good. (absolutely / very)
2 Luckily, the instructions were _____ easy to understand. (completely / fairly)
3 Tanya was _____ furious with Mario. (utterly / slightly)
4 The band's latest record turned out to be _____ popular. (extremely / totally)
5 It's _____ impossible to find a room in Edinburgh at this time of the year. (virtually / very)
6 Are you _____ certain that Daniel hasn't been in today? (rather / totally)
7 We'd go outside, but it's _____ cold today. (absolutely / extremely)
8 The train fair to London is _____ cheap at weekends. (utterly / reasonably)

7 Complete the sentences with the adjectives in the correct order.
1 I certainly don't like my shirt. It has five _____ _____ buttons. (green ugly plastic)
2 Johanna should definitely throw away her _____ _____ bicycle. (old rusty)
3 My dad is always happy when he is wearing a _____ _____ sweater. (woolen comfortable)
4 My uncle Graham has an expensive taste for _____ _____ cars. (Italian fast sports)
5 Look at that baby's _____ eyes! (brown round big)
6 I'm looking for a _____ jacket. (leather black new)

Vocabulary

Phrasal verbs

8 Match the phrasal verbs with their meanings.

1. hit it off
2. make for
3. make out
4. make up
5. pay off
6. see off
7. set off
8. set up

a to go towards a place
b to say goodbye to someone at an airport, station, etc
c to start a journey
d to say something that isn't true
e to be able to see or hear something with difficulty
f to get on well with somebody on first meeting them
g to organise and establish something
h to return all the money you owe somebody

9 Complete the sentences with the correct form of the phrasal verbs from 8.

1. If you listen hard, you can just _____ the sound of music in the distance.
2. We _____ the twins at the airport yesterday.
3. When he finished university, he _____ his own software company.
4. She walked out of the hotel and _____ the beach.
5. I don't know if I'll ever be able to _____ my student loan.
6. What time shall we _____ for the station tomorrow?
7. When Harry and Susan met, they really _____ – and now they're married!
8. I don't believe you. I think you are _____ it _____.

Prepositions

10 Circle the correct words.

1. We were **at / by / with** sea for four weeks, and I was getting tired of it.
2. 2,000 miles is a long way to travel **at / by / with** car.
3. I think there's something wrong **at / by / with** you if you don't like going to the beach.
4. That was **at / by / with** far the best meal we have had so far this holiday.
5. He was stopped by the police driving down the motorway **at / by / with** 120 mph.
6. I had to go to hospital **at / by / with** food poisoning on the first day of the holiday.

Collocations & Expressions

11 Complete the sentences with these words.

private   progress   return   run   rush   stock

1. I'm sorry, Sir – we don't have any red T-shirts in _____ at the moment.
2. Is there somewhere we can speak in _____? I have something important to tell you.
3. Why are you in such a _____? We've got plenty of time.
4. I think that you made the right decision, because it will work out for the best in the long _____.
5. The redecoration of the classroom is in _____ – it should be finished by the end of the month.
6. OK, I'll help you with this – but you'll have to do something for me in _____.

Unit 22

Words easily confused

12 Use the words given to complete the sentences underneath. Make sure the words are in the correct form. Use each word at least once.

1. know   realize   recognise   understand
   a. Although I hadn't seen her for 30 years, I _____ her immediately.
   b. I don't _____ what his name is.
   c. It wasn't until I saw the photograph that I _____ who she was.
   d. In order to _____ the theory, you need to have considerable mathematical ability.

2. advantage   benefit   exploitation   profit
   a. You shouldn't take _____ of her good nature.
   b. We expect to make a large _____ on the deal.
   c. The _____ of developing countries by the West is nothing new.
   d. Free life insurance is just one of the _____ offered by the company.

3. alive   live   lively   living
   a. My oldest _____ relative is 88 years old.
   b. The match will be shown _____ at ten o'clock.
   c. When the rescue team found her, she was still _____.
   d. Having _____ children around the house is exhausting but fun.

4. pollute   rot   spoil   stain
   a. They _____ the whole evening by insulting everyone they spoke to.
   b. I'm afraid the drink you spilt has _____ the carpet.
   c. As the wooden window frames had _____ we replaced them.
   d. If we go on _____ the rivers, all living things in them will die.

Word formation mixed

13 Use the word in capitals to form a word that fits in the gap.

1. Please be careful when driving on _____ roads. — **ICE**
2. My CD collection is arranged _____. — **ALPHABET**
3. His ambition is to have a successful career in _____. — **JOURNAL**
4. What a strange _____ meeting you here! — **COINCIDE**
5. We had a(n) _____ wet April this year – in fact, it was the wettest on record. — **USUAL**
6. I think it is _____ to tell lies to children, so I never do it. — **MORAL**
7. We had to _____ the entire first scene because the director didn't like the first version. — **WRITE**
8. She stared at her _____ in the mirror. — **REFLECT**

Sentence transformation

14 Complete the second sentence so that it has a similar meaning to the first sentence, using the word given. Do not change the word given. You must use between two and five words.

1 She can't go away on holiday alone because she is too young.
   old
   She _____ to go away on holiday on her own.

2 This is such a brilliant book that I don't want it to end.
   so
   This book _____ that I don't want it to end.

3 You are not qualified for this job.
   qualifications
   You don't _____ for this job.

4 Your sister is so clever.
   such
   You have _____ sister.

5 They got on very well when they met.
   hit
   They _____ when they met.

6 Let's head in the direction of the hills.
   make
   Let's _____ the hills.

7 He hurries wherever he goes.
   rush
   He is _____ wherever he goes.

8 I think he invented the whole story.
   up
   I think _____ the whole story.

Unit 22 155

Unit 23

Awareness

1 Which of these sentences are correct (C) and incorrect (I)?

1 I wish I know how to speak Spanish. ___
2 If only you hadn't lost your address book. ___
3 You'd better to go to bed now. ___
4 It's about time I went home. ___
5 I'd much rather to stay at home tonight. ___
6 Would you prefer to live in the country? ___
7 I rather eat an apple than a banana. ___
8 I wish I could fly. ___
9 She prefers junk food. ___
10 If only you weren't so stubborn. ___

How many did you get right? ☐

Grammar

Wish & If only

We use *wish* to talk about a situation or an action we aren't happy about, or to say how we would like something to be different.

We use *wish* + a past tense when we talk about the present or the future.
I **wish** I **knew** how to do karate.

We use *wish* + a past perfect tense when we talk about the past.
I **wish** I **hadn't slept** for so long this morning.

We use *wish* + *would* + bare infinitive when we talk about other people's annoying habits or to say that we would like something to be different in the future. We use it for actions, not states. We can only use *wish* + *would* when the subjects are different.
I **wish** they **would let** children into pubs.
I **wish** the price of petrol **would go** down.

We can use *if only* instead of *wish* in affirmative and negative sentences.
If only I didn't have a broken arm.
If only I hadn't lost my invitation.

Had Better

We generally use *had better* to give advice for a specific situation in the present or future. It is followed by the bare infinitive.
You'**d better ask** the head teacher for permission.

> **Note**
> *Had better* is sometimes used to make threats.
> You'**d better** do as you are told or you won't be allowed out this weekend.

It's (about/high) time

We can use *it's time*, *it's about time* and *it's high time* + past tense to talk about something that should have already been done in the present.
It's time you started a proper exercise program.
It's about time you learnt how to use a computer.
It's high time Tim stopped eating junk food.

Would Rather

We use *would rather* to show a preference in the present or future. We use *would rather* + bare infinitive when we are talking about ourselves.
I'**d rather go** to a café than cook breakfast.

We use *would rather* followed by a pronoun and a past tense when we are talking about somebody else in the present or future.
'Shall we go to the cinema this evening?' 'No, I'**d rather we went** to a club.'

Would Prefer & Prefer

We use *would prefer* to show preference in a particular situation (not in general). We can use
- *would prefer* + noun.
'Would you like to play tennis or football?' '*I'd prefer tennis.*'
- *would prefer* + full infinitive.
I'd prefer to ride my bike.
- *would prefer* + full infinitive + *rather than* + bare infinitive.
I'd prefer to visit grandma rather than stay at home.

We use *prefer* to show preference in general. We can use
- *prefer* + noun.
I prefer athletics (to other sports).
- *prefer* + full infinitive + *than* + bare infinitive.
I prefer to run than walk.
- *prefer* + -ing + to + -ing.
I prefer reading a good book to watching TV.

> **Note**
> We can also use *prefer* with *rather*.
> *I prefer to run rather than walk.*

Grammar Exercises

2 Circle the correct words.

1. My mother wishes she **can / could** type faster.
2. I wish I **spoke / speak** French.
3. She wishes she **learnt / had learnt** Spanish when she was much younger.
4. I have put on a lot of weight. If only I **didn't eat / hadn't eaten** so much at Christmas.
5. If only I **could go / went** on holiday next month.
6. I wish I **bought / had bought** that car a year ago.
7. James wishes he **didn't sleep / hadn't slept** on the beach. Now he's sunburnt.
8. I wish Mary **doesn't drive / didn't drive** so fast.
9. They wish I **came / had come** home earlier last night.
10. If only I **could come / came** with you tomorrow.

3 Complete the sentences with the word that best fits each gap.

1. I _____ I knew how to dance.
2. If _____ I had met her years ago.
3. You _____ better not be lying to me.
4. It's about _____ you learnt how to cook.
5. I'd _____ cook pasta than boil rice.
6. Do you prefer _____ spend time with family or friends?
7. I prefer to relax at home rather _____ do tiring sports.

4 Complete the sentences with **had better** or **would rather**.

1. You _____ get changed out of those wet clothes.
2. You _____ ask the teacher to explain it to you.
3. I _____ go to a football match than a basketball match.
4. You _____ be a police officer than a firefighter, wouldn't you?
5. I _____ get this homework finished or I'll be in trouble.
6. Your brother _____ not have lost my bike!
7. To be honest, I _____ not play with you if you are going to cheat.
8. You _____ tell me the truth!

Unit 23

5 Complete the sentences with the correct form of the verbs in brackets.

1. If only I _____ (have) more money. I would like to buy that camera.
2. She wishes she _____ (study) medicine when she had the chance.
3. My father wishes he _____ (buy) that house last year. Now it's much more expensive.
4. I wish I _____ (study). I can't concentrate.
5. I wish you _____ (turn) the volume down a little. I am trying to work.
6. Martin wishes I _____ (not tell) everybody his secret.
7. I wish I _____ (do) my homework yesterday. Now I'll have to stay up late.
8. He wishes he _____ (come) to the party last Saturday.
9. Jack wishes he _____ (not eat) so much. Now he feels awful.
10. I wish our neighbours _____ (stop) shouting. I can't sleep.

6 Complete the sentences to give advice using the correct form of these verbs and **It's time**.

| buy   cut   go   grow   have   wash |

1. 'My car is very dirty.'
   '_____It's time you washed_____ it.'
2. 'The grass is really long in our garden.'
   '_____ it.'
3. 'My computer is eight years old.'
   '_____ a new one.'
4. 'I've been working too hard recently.'
   '_____ on holiday.'
5. 'My hair is too long.'
   '_____ it cut.'
6. 'John is acting like a child.'
   '_____ up.'

7 Find the mistakes and correct the sentences where necessary. Put a tick (✓) below those which do not need correcting.

1. I'd prefer eat in tonight.
   _____

2. Do you prefer swimming or surfing?
   _____

3. I prefer healthy food fast food.
   _____

4. He'd prefer to sleep on the floor rather sleep on the sofa.
   _____

5. I prefer dancing to sing.
   _____

6. Would you prefer to go alone?
   _____

158

Vocabulary

Phrasal verbs

8 Match the phrasal verbs with their meanings.

1. bring up
2. clear up
3. come down with
4. come round
5. come up with
6. pull up
7. stand up for
8. turn up

a to get an illness
b to arrive somewhere
c to become conscious again
d to begin to talk about a particular subject
e (of a vehicle) to stop by the road side temporarily
f to think of an idea
g to make tidy
h to defend something or somebody from attack

9 Complete the sentences with the correct form of the phrasal verbs from 8.

1. We didn't know what to do until George _____ a brilliant idea.
2. A car _____ next to me while I was waiting for a bus – it was my uncle.
3. Don't forget to _____ the subject of the school fair at the next meeting.
4. I _____ the flu on the first day of the summer holidays.
5. When he _____, he was lying on the pavement surrounded by people.
6. His big sister always _____ him in the playground, so he never got bullied.
7. Can you _____ this mess before your mother gets home, please?
8. We were very surprised when the Barkers _____ at our house on Sunday morning.

Prepositions

10 Circle the correct words.

1. By the time I saw the dentist I was **in / under / up** agony.
2. You ought to take up a sport, because you are **in / under / up** really bad shape at the moment.
3. After three weeks in bed, my grandmother was finally **in / under / up** and about.
4. If you're feeling **in / under / up** the weather, why not take the day off?
5. Children are **in / under / up** a lot of pressure to succeed at school these days.
6. Someone was riding a motorbike **in / under / up** and down the street late last night.

Collocations & Expressions

11 Complete the sentences with the correct form of these verbs.

| apply   catch   lose   make   skip   take |

1. You'll _____ a cold if you go out without a scarf.
2. Take this cream and _____ it to your cut.
3. I was late, so I _____ breakfast and went straight to school.
4. Lie down and I'll _____ your temperature.
5. Fortunately, Sara _____ a full recovery from her illness.
6. Sorry, I can't eat this – I've completely _____ my appetite.

Unit 23 159

Unit 23

Words easily confused

12 Use the words given to complete the sentences underneath. Make sure the words are in the correct form. Use each word at least once.

1. contest event game match
   a. I'm not in the mood for a _____ of cards.
   b. After winning a talent _____, she appeared on national television.
   c. The flower show is the village's most popular annual _____.
   d. Several football _____ had to be postponed due to heavy snow.

2. crest lid peak top
   a. There was a crow's nest at the _____ of the tree.
   b. The surfer stayed on the _____ of a wave for a few seconds before falling into the water.
   c. At the _____ of her career, she earned vast sums of money.
   d. He couldn't get the _____ off the biscuit tin.

3. direct immediate instant straight
   a. There are no _____ flights to Washington from this airport.
   b. She was so tired that she went _____ to bed.
   c. The residents cut off by the floods are in no _____ danger.
   d. I haven't got enough _____ coffee to make us all a cup.

4. chop grate peel slice
   a. Could you _____ some cheese to put on the spaghetti, please?
   b. I can never _____ a potato without wasting half of it.
   c. _____ the parsley on this board, will you?
   d. They'll _____ the ham for you at the supermarket.

Word formation noun → adjective

13 Use the word in capitals to form a word that fits in the gap.

1. You look _____ in that pirate costume. **RIDICULE**
2. We cycle more than we drive because it is more _____. **ECOLOGY**
3. That film has a very _____ ending. **DRAMA**
4. I have never had such a _____ toothache in my life! **PAIN**
5. We found a _____ old bike at the bottom of the garden. **RUST**
6. He didn't expect his business to be very _____, but it was. **PROFIT**
7. It is not a good idea to set up a factory in a _____ area. **RESIDENT**
8. You don't have to study a language here – it's _____. **OPTION**

Sentence transformation

14 Complete the second sentence so that it has a similar meaning to the first sentence, using the word given. Do not change the word given. You must use between two and five words.

1 Your bedroom really needs to be painted.
   high
   It's _____ was painted.

2 'I highly recommend you stop smoking,' the doctor told me.
   better
   The doctor said _____ stop smoking.

3 Going to the park would be better than doing homework.
   rather
   I _____ to the park than do homework.

4 Susan thinks it's better to ride than to walk.
   prefers
   Susan _____ walking.

5 Greg is always protected by his best friend.
   stands
   Greg's best friend _____ him.

6 I caught a cold on my first day of school.
   down
   I _____ on my first day of school.

7 Mum is finally able to get out of bed again.
   about
   Mum is finally _____ again.

8 You are always tired because of your poor physical condition.
   shape
   You are _____, which is why you are always tired.

Unit 24

Awareness

1 Which of these sentences are correct (C) and incorrect (I)?

1. He's getting use to living alone. ___
2. Not only did he win, but he also broke the record. ___
3. I'm not used having a cooked breakfast. ___
4. Never she had seen such a boring film. ___
5. Under no circumstances are you allowed in here. ___
6. Seldom you see a bear in a suit. ___
7. Little did he know the police were waiting for him. ___
8. No sooner we had got home than the electricity went off. ___
9. Only then did he realise his mistake. ___
10. I've been getting used to the new computer system. ___

How many did you get right? ☐

Grammar

Be Used To & Get Used To

We use *be used to* + gerund/noun to talk about actions and states which are usual or familiar.
Andy **is used to working** at night because he has been doing it for ages.

We use *get used to* + gerund/noun to talk about actions and states which are becoming more familiar.
The students **are getting used to the** new head teacher's **rules**.

Note

Be and *get* change depending on the tense that is needed in the context.

I **was used to hot weather** because I had been living in Egypt for many years.
I **have been getting used to** going to bed early.

Inversion

We can use certain words and expressions at the beginning of a sentence for emphasis. When we do this, the word order changes. This is called inversion.
Steven has never seen a shooting star.
Never has Steven seen a shooting star.
Jake not only fixes computers, he makes them.
Not only does Jake fix computers, **but he also** makes them.
You are not allowed to smoke here under any circumstances.
Under no circumstances are you allowed to smoke here.
We had no idea that the hotel would be so busy.
Little did we know that the hotel would be so busy.
You rarely/seldom see old people with MP3 players.
Rarely/Seldom do you see old people with MP3 players.
The teacher didn't offer to help me once with my project.
Not once did the teacher offer to help me with my project.
We didn't realise the dog was ill until we got home.
Only when we got home did we realise the dog was ill.
It started to rain when we hung the clothes out to dry.
No sooner had we hung the clothes out to dry **when** it started to rain.

Note

We can also invert some conditional forms. The inverted form replaces the *if*-clause.

Had I known about the party, I would have come. (If I had known about the party, I would have come.)
Should you want to freshen up, the bathroom is on the first floor. (If you want to freshen up, the bathroom is on the first floor.)

Grammar Exercises

2 Circle the correct words.
1. I'm not used to **tell / telling** other people what to do.
2. He **isn't used to / didn't use to** driving such a big car.
3. Graham **wasn't used to / didn't use to** the routine when he first arrived.
4. Have you **got / been** used to living in the city yet?
5. I could never get used to **staying / stay** out so late.
6. She has great difficulty in **being / getting** used to living alone.
7. He will soon get used to **tidy / tidying** his own room.
8. My sister **gets / is** used to doing her homework in the morning.

3 Complete the sentences with the correct form of be/get used to.
1. I find it difficult to _____ driving on the left. I think it will take me some time.
2. Mark will never _____ learning history by heart. He finds it difficult.
3. The students _____ studying hard as their teacher is very demanding.
4. I _____ having orange juice and eggs for breakfast.
5. His parents (not) _____ eating out every night.
6. I could _____ living in a luxury apartment like this.
7. Your dad will soon _____ eating healthily.
8. She (not) _____ working so late into the night.

4 Combine the sentences with Not only ..., but ... also.
1. They spent a month in Bali. They also spent a month in the Bahamas.
   _____
2. She owns a large flat in the city. She has a villa in the country, too.
   _____
3. She had been spying on the foreign diplomat. She had also given him false information.
   _____
4. The car is very fast. It is safe too.
   _____
5. It was very cold. There was also a strong wind.
   _____
6. He's a great guitarist. He's a brilliant songwriter, too.
   _____

5 Choose the correct beginning for the sentences.
1. ____ has Barry won a race.
   a Never b Little c Not only
2. ____ had we sat down to eat than the baby started to cry.
   a Only then b Hardly c Had
3. ____ are dogs allowed in the shop.
   a No sooner b Little c Under no circumstances
4. ____ did I know they had set a trap for me.
   a Not only b Little c No sooner
5. ____ he been informed, he would have acted differently.
   a Seldom b Only c Had
6. ____ did anyone ask why I was there.
   a Not only b Not once c Little

Unit 24 163

Unit 24

6 Invert the sentences.

1 I have never had such a great time.
Never _____.

2 You may not, under any circumstances, leave the room while the exam is in progress.
Under no _____.

3 She had no idea that there was a surprise party waiting for her when she got home.
Little _____.

4 You rarely see a policeman on a bicycle these days.
Rarely _____.

5 She did not stop once for a rest.
Not once _____.

6 As soon as I shut the door I realised my keys were still inside.
No sooner _____.

7 If she had remembered her umbrella, she would have stayed dry.
Had _____.

7 Complete the sentences with the word that best fits each gap.

1 I'm not used _____ waking up at 4 am.
2 _____ no circumstances is anyone allowed into this room.
3 Not _____ does he play football, but he also plays tennis.
4 Little _____ we suspect that our tour guide was actually a thief.
5 Only _____ did I discover who my true father was.
6 _____ you asked for permission first, nobody would have objected.

Vocabulary

Phrasal verbs

8 Match the phrasal verbs with their meanings.

1 break off ☐   a to remove something
2 cut off ☐   b to suddenly end
3 fight off ☐   c to lose consciousness
4 pass away ☐   d to slowly stop having an effect
5 pass on ☐   e to die
6 pass out ☐   f to tell someone something that another person has told you
7 take away ☐   g to resist
8 wear off ☐   h to make isolated

9 Complete the sentences with the correct form of the phrasal verbs from 8.

1 The flood waters rose so high that our whole village was _____ from the rest of the country.
2 When you tell Maria the news, you can be sure she'll _____ it _____ to everyone.
3 They _____ their engagement after having a big argument.
4 It was so hot that day that many of the spectators _____, and had to be taken to hospital.
5 My grandfather _____ at the age of 87.
6 There are many different drugs you can take to _____ the flu these days.
7 As the effects of the painkillers _____, I became more and more uncomfortable.
8 My parents _____ my laptop as punishment for failing all of my exams.

164

Prepositions

10 Circle the correct words.
1 Are you allergic for / from / to dairy products?
2 Perhaps he will benefit for / from / to a course of vitamin tablets.
3 If you have had all your vaccinations, you should be immune for / from / to all the major childhood diseases.
4 It didn't take long for Rosie to get sick of / from / to the hospital food.
5 Fortunately, I don't suffer for / from / to any allergies.
6 A lack of / from / to vitamin C is the reason why your teeth bleed when you brush them.

Collocations & Expressions

11 Complete the sentences with the correct form of these verbs.

  seize   shake   slam   slide   splash   sweep

1 The door to the hotel lobby _____ open automatically when we approached.
2 You should _____ the opportunity to go to university.
3 The children were happily _____ around in the swimming pool.
4 He came into the room and _____ his bag down on the table, shouting at the top of his voice.
5 'No, I cannot understand this,' she said, _____ her head sadly.
6 We left the tent on the beach, and by the morning it had been _____ away by the waves.

Words easily confused

12 Use the words given to complete the sentences underneath. Make sure the words are in the correct form. Use each word at least once.

1   base   bed   bottom   end
  a Apparently, there is a lot of treasure lying on the sea _____.
  b There must be several unknown species living at the _____ of the ocean.
  c The statue stands on a marble _____.
  d Many people have predicted the _____ of the world.

2   earlier   former   past   previous
  a As a(n) _____ prime minister, she has many important contacts.
  b We should have caught a(n) _____ flight.
  c How much _____ experience have you had?
  d She's not been well for the _____ few days.

3   close   draw   shut   turn off
  a Talks are going smoothly and we hope to _____ the deal this evening.
  b _____ the radio for a moment.
  c Please _____ the door on the way out.
  d When it gets dark, _____ the curtains.

4   complete   total   whole
  a It took three _____ weeks to repair the robot.
  b They won't stop until the work is _____.
  c The _____ number of students present is 91.
  d I'll give you £50 for the _____ lot.
  e These volumes contain the _____ works of Shakespeare.
  f You must tell the _____ truth.

Unit 24

Word formation mixed

13 Use the word in capitals to form a word that fits in the gap.

1 What a _____ dress you are wearing tonight! — COLOUR
2 His father is the _____ man in the village. — WEALTH
3 The children complained _____ throughout the entire car journey. — CONTINUE
4 Tragically, there were no _____ of the accident. — SURVIVE
5 I couldn't get rid of the horrible feeling of _____ I had since I woke up. — SICK
6 Germs enter your blood _____, and that is how you catch the disease. — VISIBLE
7 The centre of the town has remained _____ for hundreds of years. — CHANGE
8 He is an imaginative child, but he sometimes has difficulty in distinguishing _____ from fantasy. — REAL

Sentence transformation

14 Complete the second sentence so that it has a similar meaning to the first sentence, using the word given. Do not change the word given. You must use between two and five words.

1 It only hurts when I laugh.
 does
 Only _____ hurt.

2 You seldom see three-wheeled cars these days.
 do
 Seldom _____ three-wheeled cars these days.

3 Animals are never allowed in the hotel rooms.
 circumstances
 Under _____ allowed in the hotel rooms.

4 As soon as we switched off the lights, the music started.
 sooner
 No _____ the lights than the music started.

5 You will grow accustomed to wearing boots.
 used
 You _____ wearing boots.

6 Our dog died last night.
 away
 Our dog _____ last night.

7 As time passes, the effects of the drug will become weaker.
 wear
 The effects of the drug _____ as time passes.

8 These pills will do you good.
 benefit
 You _____ these pills.

Review 6

B2 Practice: FCE

Part 1

For questions 1–12, read the text below and decide which answer (A, B, C or D) best fits each gap. There is an example at the beginning (0).

Modern tourism

Tourism has **(0)** ___ in for a lot of criticism recently, but fortunately it has been unaffected by it. One common fault found with it is that **(1)** ___ no longer broadens the mind. But why should it? Surely, the holidaymakers who choose to go on a **(2)** ___ tour know just what such a holiday **(3)** ___. This is what **(4)** ___ to them, so why shouldn't they go on this type of holiday? Travel writers generally **(5)** ___ down on them because of their lack of adventure – 'all they want is a room with a sea **(6)** ___!' But what if they don't want broader minds? Maybe they choose these holiday **(7)** ___ because their minds can't get any broader!

Another criticism leveled at tourism concerns the changes **(8)** ___ at holiday destinations: the **(9)** ___ culture changes, land is developed, **(10)** ___ roads are built and locals perform for their guests. In other words, the tourist is **(11)** ___ with a copy of the place he or she has just left plus service. So why should there be any criticism? The world is changing rapidly and neither you nor I have the **(12)** ___ to stop it. Just sit back and enjoy the ride!

0	(A) come	B gone	C stayed	D been
1	A journey	B voyage	C travel	D expedition
2	A package	B packet	C parcel	D holiday
3	A involves	B forms	C consists	D holds
4	A draws	B pleases	C attracts	D appeals
5	A see	B look	C let	D keep
6	A sight	B vision	C scene	D view
7	A resorts	B ports	C places	D shores
8	A watched	B viewed	C observed	D glanced
9	A first	B country	C home	D native
10	A principal	B significant	C main	D chief
11	A performed	B shown	C given	D provided
12	A ability	B qualification	C skill	D talent

Review 6

Part 2

For questions 13–24, read the text below and think of the word which best fits each gap. Use only one word in each gap. There is an example at the beginning (0).

The other point of view

Very often a disagreement (0) __between__ two friends, neighbours or colleagues can lead to problems. In order to avoid falling (13) _____ with a friend, neighbour or workmate, it (14) _____ always an excellent idea to try to see the other person's point of view.

If you carefully consider how (15) _____ else thinks, your own thinking (16) _____ improve, so write down the views your friend, neighbour or colleague is likely to have. Not only will their thoughts surprise you, but you may find a solution (17) _____ the problem as well.

Recently a friend of mine bought a new printer. The dealer in the shop had recommended it, but she was let (18) _____ when she found out it was no better than her old one. (19) _____ taking it back, she (20) _____ a thought. She realised that if the dealer was criticised, he (21) _____ be offended. So, instead of complaining, she said that she had (22) _____ a mistake by not asking for the right printer. The dealer changed it free of charge.

If my friend (23) _____ not handled the problem in this way, the dealer would not have provided her (24) _____ a free replacement.

Part 3

For questions 25–34, read the text below. Use the word given in capitals at the end of each line to form a word that fits in the gap in the same line. There is an example at the beginning (0).

A stressful time

Life is stressful for all of us sometimes. However, most of us would agree that the most
(0) __confusing__ time in a person's life is adolescence. It is a time when   **CONFUSE**
(25) _____ that will affect a person's future have to be made.   **CHOOSE**
Perhaps this is (26) _____, because it is also the time when   **FORTUNE**
teenagers are so distracted by other things that they may not be capable of making
such decisions. (27) _____ comes at a time when it is most   **DEPEND**
difficult to handle.
These two factors, together with the constant pressure to be academically
(28) _____, can mean that sometimes teenagers behave   **SUCCESS**
badly when they are subject to (29) _____. All too often adults   **CRITIC**
regard those in their teens as being (30) _____, and make   **THINK**
continuous (31) _____ about their attitude towards older   **COMPLAIN**
people. Yet, if an adult under stress behaves (32) _____ at any   **NATURAL**
time, things are different. (33) _____ from an adult, for example,   **RUDE**
may be excused because they are under pressure. Why is this? People tend to lose
(34) _____ of the fact that adolescents are also under great   **SEE**
pressure when going through this difficult time of their lives.

Part 4

For questions 35–42, complete the second sentence so that it has a similar meaning to the first sentence, using the word given. Do not change the word given. You must use between two and five words, including the word given. Here is an example (0).

Example:

0 Fix it now or it will get worse.
otherwise
You'd _____*better fix it now otherwise*_____ it will get worse.

35 There's no need to shout.
voice
Please _____ down.

36 Many people think that scientists have received signals from alien life forms.
thought
Scientists _____ signals from alien life forms.

37 Taking care of four young children is difficult.
look
It isn't _____ four young children.

38 We enjoyed ourselves at the dance.
time
We _____ at the dance.

39 What they need to do is form a new committee.
ought
They really _____ up a new committee.

40 Be very quiet and you can watch me repair the clock.
long
You can watch me repair the clock _____ very quiet.

41 Let me see your drawing.
look
Let me have _____ you have drawn.

42 He drew cartoons before he began making films.
worked
He _____ before he began making films.

Review 6

B2 Practice: ECCE

Grammar

For questions 1–20 choose the word or phrase that best completes the sentence or conversation.

1 I'm not as sporty ___ you.
 A as
 B like
 C than
 D for

2 You ___ ask your mother about this.
 A would better
 B had better
 C are better
 D have better

3 'You look exhausted.'
 'I'm not ___ up so late.'
 A used to staying
 B used to stay
 C getting used to stay
 D getting to staying

4 If only he ___ about the new rules.
 A knows
 B is knowing
 C had known
 D have known

5 The further he ran, the ___ he became.
 A more tired
 B tireder
 C most tired
 D tiredest

6 'Why don't you join the club?'
 'I'm not ___.'
 A enough old
 B too old
 C old enough
 D old too

7 'I hate these shoes!'
 'You'll ___ to them.'
 A be used
 B get used
 C be using
 D get using

8 'Look at that photograph.'
 'It's ___ beautiful.'
 A such
 B so
 C enough
 D much

9 The film was ___ good.
 A absolutely
 B totally
 C utterly
 D extremely

10 Do you like my ___ bag?
 A blue new school
 B new blue school
 C new school blue
 D blue school new

11 Rarely ___ abroad on holiday.
 A we do go
 B go we
 C do we go
 D we go

12 He's the ___ man I know.
 A braver
 B bravest
 C most brave
 D more brave

13 'I can't swim.'
 'It's ___ time you learnt!'
 A high
 B low
 C tall
 D around

14 I prefer ___ than take public transport.
 A driving
 B drive
 C driven
 D to drive

15 'Did you enjoy that?'
 'It was ___ ride ever!'
 A the excitingest
 B the more exciting
 C the exciting
 D the most exciting

16 ___ there been such a celebration in this house!
 A There never
 B Has ever
 C Never has
 D Has never

17 'Shall we go out?'
 'I ___ stay in.'
 A 'd rather
 B 've rather
 C 'm rather
 D 'll rather

18 You're ___ baby!
 A such a
 B so
 C such
 D so a

19 Not ___ do they misbehave, but they won't eat either.
 A just
 B solely
 C alone
 D only

20 We arrived later ___ anyone.
 A as
 B like
 C than
 D for

Vocabulary

For questions 21–40, choose the word or phrase that most appropriately completes the sentence.

21 I like to ___ out in the gym three times a week.
   A check
   B work
   C pull
   D figure

22 You shouldn't ___ breakfast, because it's an important meal.
   A jump
   B skip
   C leap
   D hop

23 A war has ___ out in northern Africa.
   A won
   B snapped
   C banged
   D broken

24 Why do we always have to stand in ___ for ages in this place?
   A line
   B queue
   C row
   D wait

25 Daniel ___ up with a brilliant idea last night.
   A went
   B ran
   C pulled
   D came

26 I'm already sick ___ boiled eggs for breakfast.
   A from
   B to
   C of
   D about

27 He ___ down the telephone in anger.
   A bashed
   B crashed
   C slammed
   D pushed

28 I ___ the opportunity as soon as it came up.
   A seized
   B held
   C arrested
   D caught

29 He really hit it ___ at the party last night.
   A out
   B off
   C on
   D in

30 I couldn't ___ what the words said.
   A make out
   B make off
   C make up
   D make over

31 How long were you ___ sea for?
   A on
   B in
   C by
   D at

32 She passed ___ in fright at the sight of the shark.
   A out
   B off
   C under
   D up

33 He ___ up this company at the age of 20.
   A made
   B did
   C put
   D set

34 I hope you have booked us ___ a nice hotel.
   A up
   B into
   C over
   D in

35 When did you come ___ with this cold?
   A down
   B up
   C over
   D across

36 It's a long way to walk, but it's ___ cycling distance.
   A in
   B with
   C within
   D on

37 Can I talk to you in ___?
   A private
   B silence
   C alone
   D solo

38 Call a doctor. I'm ___ agony.
   A under
   B with
   C in
   D on

39 That horrible photograph has made me ___ my appetite.
   A throw
   B lose
   C miss
   D fail

40 I'm trying to ___ off the flu at the moment, but I'm not succeeding.
   A push
   B battle
   C box
   D fight

Irregular verbs

Infinitive	Past Simple	Past Participle
be	was/were	been
beat	beat	beaten
become	became	become
bite	bit	bitten
blow	blew	blown
break	broke	broken
bring	brought	brought
broadcast	broadcast	broadcast
build	built	built
burn	burnt	burnt
buy	bought	bought
can	could	–
catch	caught	caught
choose	chose	chosen
come	came	come
cost	cost	cost
cut	cut	cut
deal	dealt	dealt
do	did	done
draw	drew	drawn
dream	dreamt	dreamt
drink	drank	drunk
drive	drove	driven
eat	ate	eaten
fall	fell	fallen
feed	fed	fed
feel	felt	felt
fight	fought	fought
find	found	found
fly	flew	flown
forbid	forbade	forbidden
forget	forgot	forgotten
freeze	froze	frozen
get	got	got
give	gave	given
go	went	gone
grow	grew	grown
hang	hung	hung
have	had	had
hear	heard	heard
hide	hid	hidden
hit	hit	hit
hold	held	held
hurt	hurt	hurt
keep	kept	kept
know	knew	known
learn	learnt	learnt
leave	left	left
lend	lent	lent
let	let	let

Infinitive	Past Simple	Past Participle
lie	lay	lain
light	lit	lit
lose	lost	lost
make	made	made
mean	meant	meant
meet	met	met
mow	mowed	mowed/mown
pay	paid	paid
prove	proved	proven
put	put	put
read	read [red]	read [red]
ride	rode	ridden
ring	rang	rung
run	ran	run
say	said	said
see	saw	seen
sell	sold	sold
send	sent	sent
set	set	set
shake	shook	shaken
shine	shone	shone
shoot	shot	shot
show	showed	shown
shut	shut	shut
sing	sang	sung
sit	sat	sat
sleep	slept	slept
slide	slid	slid
smell	smelt	smelt
speak	spoke	spoken
spend	spent	spent
spoil	spoilt	spoilt
spread	spread	spread
stand	stood	stood
steal	stole	stolen
stick	stuck	stuck
stink	stank	stunk
swim	swam	swum
take	took	taken
teach	taught	taught
tear	tore	torn
tell	told	told
think	thought	thought
throw	threw	thrown
understand	understood	understood
wake	woke	woken
wear	wore	worn
win	won	won
write	wrote	written

Phrasal verbs

back up	=	to make a spare copy of something on a computer	(U9)
beaver away	=	to work hard at something	(U15)
believe in	=	to be sure that something is right	(U12)
block out	=	to stop light or noise passing through	(U15)
blow over	=	(of a storm or argument) to end without causing harm	(U15)
blow up	=	to destroy with a bomb	(U15)
book into	=	to arrange for a room in a hotel	(U21)
bottle up	=	to hide strong emotions	(U2)
break down	=	to suddenly stop working	(U9)
break into	=	to illegally enter a building	(U21)
break off	=	to suddenly end	(U24)
break out	=	(of something unpleasant) to suddenly start	(U21)
breeze through	=	to succeed easily	(U19)
bring up	=	to begin to talk about a particular subject	(U23)
brush up	=	to improve a skill	(U19)
burn out	=	to become too ill or tired to do any more work	(U2)
burst into	=	to suddenly start	(U15)
burst into	=	to suddenly start making a noise, especially laughing or crying	(U2)
call someone back	=	to telephone someone again	(U3)
call for	=	to require or demand	(U4)
call in	=	to visit for a short time usually while on the way to another place	(U4)
call off	=	to cancel an event	(U3)
call on	=	to ask	(U4)
call out	=	to shout	(U4)
call round	=	to visit someone's house	(U3)
call up	=	to telephone	(U3)
calm down	=	to become less excited	(U2)
catch on	=	to become popular	(U5)
catch up	=	to reach someone in front of you by moving faster than them	(U5)
cater to	=	to provide something that is wanted	(U5)
check in	=	to arrive and register at a hotel or airport	(U21)
check out	=	to pay the bill and leave a hotel	(U21)
check up on	=	to find out how someone or something is progressing	(U21)
cheer up	=	to feel happier, or make someone feel happier	(U1)
chicken out	=	to become too afraid to do something	(U2)
chill out	=	to relax	(U1)
clam up	=	to refuse to say anything	(U15)
clear up	=	to make tidy	(U23)
come across	=	to discover by accident	(U3)
come along	=	to go somewhere with someone	(U3)
come down	=	to become lower (in price)	(U3)
come down with	=	to catch (a disease), to get an illness	(U5, U23)
come in for	=	to receive (criticism or praise)	(U5)
come out	=	(of information) to become available or known	(U4)
come out	=	to become available to buy	(U3)
come round	=	to become conscious again	(U23)
come to	=	to total, when added together	(U4)
come up	=	to be mentioned in a conversation	(U4)
come up with	=	to suggest an idea or plan	(U4)
come up with	=	to think of an idea	(U23)

cut down	=	to reduce the amount of something	(U12)
cut down on	=	to reduce the number or amount of something	(U17)
cut off	=	to make isolated	(U24)
do away with	=	to kill or get rid of	(U13)
do up	=	to fix or decorate something, so that it looks good	(U13)
do without	=	to manage without something	(U13)
drop out	=	to quit a course of study	(U19)
face up to something	=	to accept a difficult but true situation or fact	(U1)
fall for someone	=	to quickly become attracted to someone	(U1)
fall out	=	to have an argument and stop being friends	(U1)
fall through	=	to fail to happen	(U19)
feel up to	=	to be well or confident enough to do something	(U11)
fight off	=	to resist	(U24)
figure out	=	to find a solution after thinking about a problem	(U16)
figure out	=	to understand something	(U19)
fill in	=	to complete a form	(U17)
fill up	=	to make full	(U17)
finish with	=	to end a relationship	(U2)
freak out	=	to suddenly become very afraid or upset	(U2)
freeze over	=	(of surface of water) to turn to ice	(U16)
get across	=	to succeed in making someone understand something	(U8)
get at	=	to be able to reach something	(U8)
get away	=	to go on holiday or a break	(U7)
get away with	=	to escape punishment for doing something wrong	(U11)
get carried away	=	to get too excited about something	(U1)
get down to	=	to start doing something properly	(U17)
get in	=	to be chos pted into an institution	(U8)
get on	=	to have a good relationship with	(U8)
get out of	=	to avoid doing something which you don't want to do	(U8)
get over	=	to recover from an illness or an upsetting situation	(U2)
get round to	=	to finally do something which you meant to do	(U8)
get through	=	to succeed in a competition or exam	(U8)
get together	=	to meet with socially	(U11)
get up	=	to stand up	(U8)
give away	=	to give something to someone for free	(U13)
give yourself up	=	to surrender to the police	(U13)
go ahead	=	to start	(U5)
go around	=	to circulate or spread	(U5)
go by	=	(of time) to pass	(U5)
go for	=	to try to get	(U20)
go off (something/someone)	=	to stop liking	(U1)
go over	=	to look at again, revise	(U20)
go through	=	to experience something difficult or unpleasant	(U19)
hack into	=	to illegally enter another computer system	(U9)
hand in	=	to submit work	(U20)
hand out	=	to distribute something among a group	(U20)
hang on	=	to wait for a short while	(U7)
hang out	=	to spend time with someone socially	(U7)
hang up	=	to stop a telephone conversation	(U7)

Phrasal verbs

hit it off	=	to get on well with someone on first meeting them	(U22)
hold down	=	to keep a job	(U17)
hold on	=	to wait for a short while	(U13)
hold up	=	to rob	(U13)
hook up to	=	to connect one machine to another	(U9)
horse around	=	to play in a silly or noisy way	(U15)
keep away	=	to stay far from, or stop someone from going near to something	(U17)
keep to	=	to stick with a plan	(U17)
keep up	=	to continue	(U17)
key in	=	to type something into a computer	(U10)
live for	=	to have something or someone as the most important thing in your life	(U6)
live on	=	to mainly eat a particular kind of food	(U6)
live up to	=	to be as good as expected	(U6)
log in	=	to join a computer network	(U10)
log out	=	to disconnect from a computer network	(U10)
look down on	=	to act like you are better than someone	(U6)
look into	=	to investigate or examine	(U6)
look out for	=	to try to notice something or someone	(U20)
look up	=	to find something in a list of things	(U20)
look up	=	to try to find information about something on the Internet or in a book	(U6)
look up to (someone)	=	to admire and respect	(U1)
make for	=	to go towards a place	(U22)
make out	=	to be able to see or hear something with difficulty	(U22)
make up	=	to say something that isn't true	(U22)
miss out on	=	to not do something which you would have enjoyed or benefited from	(U19)
move in	=	to begin living in a new house or flat	(U18)
move in	=	to start living in a place	(U7)
move on	=	to change the subject you are talking about	(U7)
move on	=	to start something new	(U18)
move out	=	to leave the house or flat where you live	(U18)
move out	=	to leave the place you live in	(U7)
nose about	=	to look for something which is hidden	(U6)
own up	=	to admit to doing something wrong	(U14)
pass around	=	to offer something to each person in a group	(U12)
pass away	=	to die	(U13, U24)
pass on	=	to tell someone something that another person has told you	(U24)
pass out	=	to lose consciousness	(U24)
pay off	=	to return all the money you owe someone	(U22)
pick on	=	to unfairly criticize or badly treat one person	(U20)
pick up	=	to learn by practising	(U20)
pig out	=	to eat too much food	(U16)
plug in	=	to connect a machine to an electricity supply	(U9)
pull in	=	to drive your car off the road and into a place	(U21)
pull up	=	(of a vehicle) to stop by the road side temporarily	(U23)
put away	=	to put someone in prison	(U14)
put down	=	to write someone's name on a document	(U14)
put off	=	to make someone dislike something	(U14)
put up with (something/someone)	=	to tolerate	(U1)
rat on	=	to be disloyal to someone, especially by giving away a secret	(U16)
run away	=	to leave a place secretly	(U11)
run into	=	to meet someone by chance	(U11)
run out	=	(of a supply) to completely finish or be used up	(U19)

run over	=	to hit someone with a vehicle	(U11)
see off	=	to say goodbye to someone at an airport, station, etc	(U22)
see through	=	to realise someone is trying to trick you	(U14)
see to	=	to deal with something that needs attention	(U14)
set off	=	to make an alarm ring	(U9)
set off	=	to start a journey	(U22)
set up	=	to organise and establish something	(U22)
settle down	=	to start feeling comfortable in a place	(U7)
show around	=	to show someone a place	(U11)
show off	=	to try to make other people think you are great by demonstrating your abilities	(U1)
show up	=	to arrive somewhere, usually unexpectedly	(U11)
shut down	=	to turn off a computer	(U9)
sit around	=	to stay at home being lazy	(U12)
sit back	=	to rest comfortably on a chair or sofa	(U12)
sleep in	=	to get out of bed later than usual	(U12)
stand back	=	to move a short distance from something	(U12)
stand up for	=	to defend something or someone from attack	(U23)
start out	=	to begin	(U6)
switch on	=	to turn on a computer, light, etc	(U9)
take after	=	to have similar characteristics to an older family member	(U14)
take away	=	to remove something	(U24)
take down	=	to remove something from the wall	(U18)
take in	=	to deceive someone	(U14)
take on	=	to employ staff	(U18)
take out	=	to remove money from your bank account	(U18)
take over	=	to take control	(U16)
take round	=	to walk around a place with someone	(U18)
take up	=	to fill an amount of time or space	(U18)
talk into	=	to persuade someone to do something	(U15)
turn back	=	to return the way you came from	(U10)
turn down	=	to make the volume or heat lower	(U10)
turn down	=	to reject an invitation	(U12)
turn out	=	to happen in a way that was not expected	(U10)
turn to	=	to ask someone for help or support	(U10)
turn up	=	to arrive somewhere	(U23)
turn up	=	to make the volume or heat higher	(U10)
wear away	=	to make smaller or smoother over time	(U16)
wear off	=	to slowly stop having an effect	(U24)
wear out	=	to make someone feel very tired	(U16)
wipe out	=	to cause to become extinct	(U16)
work out	=	(of something unpleasant) to suddenly start	(U21)

Prepositions

(be) accused of	(U14)	as a matter of fact	(U8)	in self-defense	(U14)
(be) against something	(U20)	as a result of something	(U7)	increase by	(U4)
(be) against the law	(U13, U20)	as far as	(U8)	keep with budget	(U10)
(be) all over the Internet	(U19)	at fault	(U4)	know all along	(U20)
(be) among something	(U7)	at least	(U11)	lack of	(U24)
(be) ashamed of	(U1)	at one's disposal	(U3)	let someone through	(U17)
(be) at loose end	(U11)	at risk of	(U4)	much to our astonishment	(U6)
(be) at sea	(U22)	attitude towards someone	(U18)	object to	(U16)
(be) at the airport	(U1)	be ashamed of	(U1)	off the coast	(U19)
(be) aware of	(U15)	behind the scenes	(U5)	on a daily basis	(U7)
(be) banned from something	(U14)	benefit from	(U24)	on account of	(U6)
(be) exposed to	(U16)	break a leg in two places	(U1)	on condition that	(U7)
(be) for real	(U12)	by all accounts	(U5)	on second thoughts	(U11)
(be) in a bad shape	(U23)	by day	(U4)	on someone's behalf	(U6)
(be) in agony	(U23)	by far	(U22)	on top of that	(U11)
(be) in favour of	(U4)	by heart	(U3)	once in a blue moon	(U11)
(be) in two minds	(U11)	campaign against	(U13)	pop over	(U17)
(be) interested in	(U2)	come at a price	(U5)	protection from	(U15)
(be) keen on	(U16)	come within	(U21)	put someone behind bars	(U5)
(be) off duty	(U19)	concentrate on	(U2)	put something in writing	(U8)
(be) on a cruise	(U21)	cope with	(U15)	rain throughout the entire holiday	(U18)
(be) on board	(U21)	deep down	(U1)		
(be) past the age	(U9)	discourage from	(U15)	rely on	(U16)
(be) promoted from	(U12)	do something along	(U9)	respond to	(U2)
(be) responsible for	(U2)	drive at (speed)	(U22)	result in	(U16)
(be) satisfied with	(U15)	feel anger towards someone	(U18)	ride up and down	(U23)
(be) thoughtful of	(U14)	feel under the weather	(U23)	speak over	(U19)
(be) under arrest	(U13)	focus on	(U2)	speak over the phone	(U9)
(be) under attack	(U17)	for a change	(U8)	stand in line	(U21)
(be) under pressure	(U23)	for the moment	(U8, U12)	start all over again	(U9)
(be) under suspicion	(U13)	from now	(U19)	suffer from	(U24)
(be) under the impression	(U1)	from time to time	(U19)	talk in private	(U5)
(be) up and about	(U23)	get on one's nerves	(U1)	threat of	(U15)
(be) within	(U21)	get sick of	(U24)	throughout the show	(U18)
(be) wrong with	(U22)	glance through	(U17)	to a lifetime	(U13)
(be) wrong with someone	(U10, U12)	go from bad to worse	(U12)	to one's mind	(U13)
a smile upon someone's face	(U18)	go to hospital with	(U22)	travel by car	(U22)
a steep rise in	(U16)	have something under control	(U6, U17)	under pressure	(U6)
a week past	(U9)	head for	(U2)	upon arrival	(U18)
advantage of something	(U7)	hide from sight	(U14)	was by far	(U3)
after all	(U20)	immune from	(U24)	win at all costs	(U3)
after something	(U20)	in connection with	(U3)	with reference to	(U12)
all over	(U17)	in exchange for	(U14)	within all that noise	(U10)
allergic to	(U24)	in general	(U3)	within the next few days	(U10)
along the road	(U20)	in public	(U5)	without a doubt	(U6)
along with something	(U9)	in search of	(U21)	without delay	(U10)
among other things	(U7)	in secret	(U8)	without taking a brake	(U10)

Collocations & Expressions

(be) a bad influence on	(U1)	do yoga	(U11)	personal space	(U8)
(be) a real pleasure + -ing	(U3)	donkey work	(U18)	pick someone's brains	(U19)
(be) absorbed in something	(U12)	excess baggage	(U21)	play a joke on someone	(U4)
(be) ashamed of something	(U12)	express my apologies to someone	(U1)	play a role	(U4)
(be) associated with something	(U12)	face doing something	(U1)	play a sport	(U11)
(be) at a loss for words	(U2)	fish for something	(U16)	play by ear	(U4)
(be) brain dead	(U19)	get on someone's nerves	(U15)	play chess	(U11)
(be) filthy rich	(U5)	get rich	(U17)	population explosion	(U8)
(be) found guilty	(U13)	get straight to the point	(U20)	put someone behind bars	(U13)
(be) in a panic	(U2)	get the feeling that	(U20)	rack one's brains	(U19)
(be) in a rush	(U22)	get the sack	(U17)	rat race	(U8, U18)
(be) in absolute agony with	(U2)	ghost town	(U7)	reach for the stars	(U5)
(be) made of money	(U6)	go bungee jumping	(U11)	save money	(U4)
(be) none of one's business	(U10)	go climbing	(U11)	save penalty	(U4)
(be) on good terms with each other	(U2)	have a lucky break	(U5)	save space	(U4)
(be) on the edge of my seat	(U2)	have something on one's brain	(U19)	seize the opportunity	(U24)
(be) under the impression	(U15)	have stars in one's eyes	(U6)	set an example	(U15)
a big name in	(U5)	home town	(U7)	sewing machine	(U9)
answering machine	(U9)	in one respect	(U15)	shake one's head	(U24)
apply a cream	(U23)	in progress	(U22)	sweep away	(U24)
at first sight	(U15)	in return	(U22)	skip breakfast	(U23)
at one's convenience	(U10)	in stock	(U22)	slam the bag	(U24)
believe my ears	(U5)	in-flight entertainment	(U21)	slide open	(U24)
beyond one's control	(U10)	jury duty	(U14)	speak in private	(U22)
boarding pass	(U21)	keep an eye on	(U6)	spend years + -ing	(U3)
brainwave	(U19)	keep one's promise	(U20)	splash around	(U24)
break one's back doing something	(U18)	keep someone amused	(U12)	take a day off	(U17)
break one's heart	(U1)	keep someone company	(U20)	take advantage of	(U13)
break the law	(U13)	know better than to do something	(U1)	take into consideration	(U10)
build a reputation	(U3)	leave someone alone	(U12)	take one's temperature	(U23)
build an empire	(U3)	let the cat out of the bag	(U16)	take one's word for something	(U20)
burglar alarm	(U14)	life sentence	(U14)	take pleasure in something	(U20)
cabin crew	(U21)	live in the fast lane	(U8)	take responsibility	(U13)
capture in a photo	(U5)	long run	(U22)	take the initiative	(U17)
cash machine	(U9)	lose one's appetite	(U23)	talk of the town	(U7)
catch a cold	(U23)	make a fool of oneself	(U1)	the brains behind something	(U19)
catch someone's attention	(U10)	make a full recovery	(U23)	the mind goes blank	(U12)
common knowledge	(U13)	make a name of oneself	(U6)	think of one's feet	(U18)
community service	(U14)	make a profit	(U17)	time machine	(U9)
concrete jungle	(U8)	make no difference	(U10)	town hall	(U7)
cook the book	(U18)	make the best of a bad situation	(U17)	value for money	(U6)
court case	(U14)	monkey business	(U18)	vending machine	(U9)
crime wave	(U14)	name drop	(U6)	walk of life	(U8)
crocodile tears	(U16)	night on the town	(U7)	washing machine	(U9)
departure gate	(U21)	out of curiosity	(U2)	with all one's heart	(U15)
do damage to	(U3)	overhead compartment	(U21)	wolf in sheep's clothing	(U16)
do karate	(U11)	paint town red	(U7)	work as a bee	(U16)
do someone good	(U3)			worm the information out of someone	(U16)

Word formation

Adjective → Adjective		
TINY	TINIEST	U10
TRICKY	TRICKIEST	U19

Adjective → Verb		
SOCIAL	SOCIALIZE	U9
SPECIAL	SPECIALIZE	U11

Adjective → Noun		
ANXIOUS	ANXIETY	U2
BRAVE	BRAVERY	U9
CONVENIENT	CONVENIENCE	U13
DIFFERENT	DIFFERENCE	U2
DISTANT	DISTANCE	U2
EQUAL	EQUALITY	U21
FIT	FITNESS	U2
FRIENDLY	UNFRIENDLINESS	U20
HONEST	DISHONESTY	U12
INTELLIGENT	INTELLIGENCE	U21
KIND	KINDNESS	U10
LAZY	LAZINESS	U18
MAD	MADNESS	U2
POPULAR	POPULARITY	U2
POWERFUL	POWER	U9
REAL	REALITY	U24
SAFE	SAFETY	U2
SICK	SICKNESS	U24
STRONG	STRENGTH	U2
TENSE	TENSION	U2
TRUE	TRUTH	U2
WEAK	WEAKNESS	U11

Adverbs		
ACCIDENT	ACCIDENTALLY	U10
ALPHABET	ALPHABETICALLY	U22
AUTOMATIC	AUTOMATICALLY	U8
CARE	CARELESSLY	U8
COMFORT	COMFORTABLY	U8
CONSCIOUS	UNCONSCIOUSLY	U8
CONTINUE	CONTINUOUSLY	U24
CONTROVERSY	CONTROVERSIALLY	U16
DANGER	DANGEROUSLY	U8
DEAD	DEADLY	U13
DELIGHT	DELIGHTFULLY	U21
EXTRAORDINARY	EXTRAORDINARILY	U8
FOOL	FOOLISHLY	U16
FURY	FURIOUSLY	U16
GENERAL	GENERALLY	U8
GUILT	GUILTILY	U16
HAPPY	HAPPILY	U11
IRRITATE	IRRITATINGLY	U16
LIKELY	UNLIKELY	U7
MEMORY	MEMORABLY	U16
OFFEND	OFFENSIVELY	U8
REPEAT	REPEATEDLY	U8
SKILL	SKILLFULLY	U16
STEADY	STEADILY	U8
SUIT	SUITABLY	U19
THOUGHT	THOUGHTFULLY	U12
TRUE	TRULY	U10
USUAL	UNUSUALLY	U22
VISIBLE	INVISIBLY	U24

Adjective → Opposite adjective		
ATTRACTIVE	UNATTRACTIVE	U7, U16
FORMAL	INFORMAL	U7
HONEST	DISHONEST	U7
LEGAL	ILLEGAL	U7
MORAL	IMMORAL	U22
ORGANISED	DISORGANISED	U7
POLITE	IMPOLITE	U7
POSSIBLE	IMPOSSIBLE	U12
REGULAR	IRREGULAR	U7
RESPONSIBLE	IRRESPONSIBLE	U7

Noun → Adjective		
ACCIDENT	ACCIDENTAL	U1
ADVENTURE	ADVENTUROUS	U20
COLOUR	COLOURFUL	U24
DOUBT	DOUBTFUL	U1
DRAMA	DRAMATIC	U23
ECOLOGY	ECOLOGICAL	U23
END	ENDLESS	U12
ENERGY	ENERGETIC	U1
FOG	FOGGY	U18
HOPE	HOPELESS	U20
ICE	ICY	U22
MEMORY	MEMORABLE	U11
MOTION	MOTIONLESS	U1
MUD	MUDDY	U21
MYSTERY	MYSTERIOUS	U1
OPTION	OPTIONAL	U23
PAIN	PAINFUL	U23
PEACE	PEACEFUL	U10
PRACTICE	PRACTICAL	U1
PRICE	PRICELESS	U21
PROFIT	PROFITABLE	U23
REASON	REASONABLE	U20
RESIDENT	RESIDENTIAL	U23
RIDICULE	RIDICULOUS	U23
RUST	RUSTY	U23
SCIENCE	SCIENTIFIC	U1
SPECTACLE	SPECTACULAR	U1
SUSPECT	SUSPICIOUS	U11
WEALTH	WEALTHIEST	U24

Noun → Noun		
BAKER	BAKERY	U6
BLOG	BLOGGERS	U6
CHAMPION	CHAMPIONSHIP	U20
CHARACTER	CHARACTERISTIC	U6
CRIME	CRIMINAL	U13
CRITIC	CRITICISM	U6
ECONOMY	ECONOMIST	U12
EXAM	EXAMINER	U6
FRIEND	FRIENDSHIP	U6
JOURNAL	JOURNALISM	U22
MEMBER	MEMBERSHIP	U11
MOTOR	MOTORISTS	U21
NATION	NATIONALITY	U6
NOVEL	NOVELIST	U19
PARTNER	PARTNERSHIP	U9
PROFESSION	PROFESSIONAL	U13
SCENE	SCENERY	U10
SCIENCE	SCIENTISTS	U6
TERROR	TERRORISM	U13
WILL	WILLINGNESS	U19

Noun → Verb		
APOLOGY	APOLOGIZE	U4
CLASS	CLASSIFY	U4
COURAGE	ENCOURAGE	U4
CRITIC	CRITICIZE	U4
PROOF	PROVE	U4
RELIEF	RELIEVE	U4
SUCCESS	SUCCEED	U4
TERROR	TERRIFY	U4

Word formation

Prefixes

ABILITY	DISABILITY	U6
ACCEPT	UNACCEPTABLE	U15
ADVANTAGE	DISADVANTAGE	U18
AGREE	DISAGREE	U12
APPEAR	DISAPPEAR	U17
APPROVE	DISAPPROVAL	U17
BREAK	UNBREAKABLE	U13
BUILD	REBUILD	U17
CHANGE	UNCHANGED	U24
CREDIBLE	INCREDIBLE	U17
EMPLOY	UNEMPLOYED	U17
EXPERIENCE	INEXPERIENCED	U15
FRIEND	UNFRIENDLY	U18
HEALTH	UNHEALTHY	U1
HELP	UNHELPFUL	U19
LIKE	DISLIKE	U11
LUCK	UNLUCKY	U9
ORDINARY	EXTRAORDINARY	U7
PATIENT	IMPATIENT	U17
PAY	REPAY	U17
SLEEP	ASLEEP	U1
SUIT	UNSUITABLE	U3
UNDERSTAND	MISUNDERSTANDING	U17
WRITE	REWRITE	U22

Verb → Adjective

ADD	ADDITIONAL	U3
AMAZE	AMAZING	U9
BENEFIT	BENEFICIAL	U19
CARE	CARELESS	U3
COMFORT	COMFORTABLE	U3
COMPETE	COMPETITIVE	U3
COOPERATE	COOPERATIVE	U15
EDUCATE	EDUCATIONAL	U15
HARM	HARMFUL	U3
HELP	HELPFUL	U15
LEAD	LEADING	U3
LEAD	MISLEADING	U20
LIKE	UNLIKEABLE	U9
LIVE	ALIVE	U10
OUTRAGE	OUTRAGEOUS	U15
RISK	RISKY	U15
SIGNIFY	SIGNIFICANT	U3
SLEEP	SLEEPY	U3
USE	USELESS	U15
VARY	VARIOUS	U3
WONDER	WONDERFUL	U18

Verb → Noun

ACT	ACTION	U6
AMAZE	AMAZEMENT	U11
ANALYSE	ANALYSIS	U5
COINCIDE	COINCIDENCE	U22
CONCLUDE	CONCLUSION	U14
CONSULT	CONSULTANT	U21
DECIDE	DECISION	U5, U14
DELIVER	DELIVERY	U18
DISCOVER	DISCOVERY	U19
EXIST	EXISTENCE	U5
GOVERN	GOVERNMENT	U9
INJURE	INJURY	U5
INSTRUCT	INSTRUCTOR	U5
JUDGE	JUDGEMENT	U18
LOSE	LOSS	U5
MAINTAIN	MAINTENANCE	U19
MOVE	MOVEMENTS	U20
OCCUPY	OCCUPATION	U14
OFFEND	OFFENCE	U13
OPERATE	OPERATION	U14
PAY	PAYMENT	U5
PERFORM	PERFORMANCE	U21
PERFORM	PERFORMERS	U9
PHOTOGRAPH	PHOTOGRAPHER	U14
PLEASE	PLEASURE	U5
PREFER	PREFERENCE	U12
PRESENT	PRESENCE	U12
PROVE	PROOF	U14
RECOMMEND	RECOMMENDATION	U14
REFER	REFERENCE	U20
REFLECT	REFLECTION	U22
RELATE	RELATIONSHIP	U18
ROB	ROBBERY	U13
SIGNIFY	SIGNIFICANCE	U14
SOLVE	SOLUTION	U5
SURVIVE	SURVIVORS	U22
VARY	VARIETY	U5

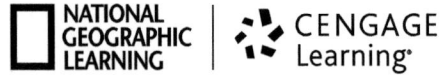

**Close-Up B2 English in Use
Student's Book**
David McKeegan

Publisher: Gavin McLean
Director of Content Development: Sarah Bideleux
Art Director: Natasa Arsenidou
Cover Designer: Tania Diakaki
Compositor: Sofia Fourtouni

Acknowledgements
Editorial and project management by hyphen SA

© 2013 National Geographic Learning, as part of Cengage Learning

ALL RIGHTS RESERVED. No part of this work covered by the copyright herein may be reproduced, transmitted, stored, or used in any form or by any means graphic, electronic, or mechanical, including but not limited to photocopying, recording, scanning, digitizing, taping, Web distribution, information networks, or information storage and retrieval systems, except as permitted under Section 107 or 108 of the 1976 United States Copyright Act, without the prior written permission of the publisher.

> For permission to use material from this text or product,
> submit all requests online at **www.cengage.com/permissions**
> Further permissions questions can be emailed to
> **permissionrequest@cengage.com**

ISBN: 978-1-4080-6162-6

National Geographic Learning
Cheriton House, North Way, Andover, Hampshire, SP10 5BE
United Kingdom

Cengage Learning is a leading provider of customized learning solutions with office locations around the globe, including Singapore, the United Kingdom, Australia, Mexico, Brazil and Japan. Locate your local office at: **international.cengage.com/region**

Cengage Learning products are represented in Canada by Nelson Education, Ltd.

Visit National Geographic Learning online at **ngl.cengage.com**

Visit our corporate website at **www.cengage.com**

Photo credits
Cover image: Shutterstock
All other images: Shutterstock

Printed in the United Kingdom by CPI Antony Rowe
Print Number: 14 Print Year: 2022